1
CHILDREN
OF GOD

THE
CHILDREN
OF GOD

MAURA HYLAND

VERITAS

First published 1989 by
Veritas Publications
7/8 Lower Abbey Street
Dublin 1

ISBN 1 85390 135 0

Cover design & typography: Eddie McManus
Typesetting by Printset & Design Ltd, Dublin
Printed in the Republic of Ireland by the Leinster Leader Ltd

CONTENTS

FOREWORD

When Boris Becker hit the final shot that gave him victory in the 1989 Wimbledon Tennis Championship, his first reaction was to fling his racquet into the stand. He didn't even look to see who caught it. He had discarded the instrument by which he had won the match — the credit was due to him — not to his racquet. His gesture forcefully underlines the fact that an instrument is only as good as the person who uses it. The catechetical programme, *The Children of God Series,* is without doubt an excellent programme, used and acclaimed throughout the English-speaking world. However, as the compilers of the programme will be the first to stress, it is just an instrument to be used in fostering the faith of the children. Its effectiveness depends on how well it is used. It is designed for use by the three partners who share responsibility for enabling the children to grow in faith, namely the parents, the teacher and the priest. To help the teacher a kit was designed which includes a teacher's manual. The pupil's book was designed as a link with the home and so it seeks to help the parents come to some understanding of the content of and processes in the programme. With the publication of this book for the priest the cycle is completed and a very real need is met. This book is meant to be an instrument in the hand of the priest as he visits, or prepares to visit the classroom.

To say this is to underline the first requirement of the priest: that is that he visit the classroom and that he do so with reasonable regularity and continuity. We all readily agree that if the parents show no interest and give no support the best efforts of the teacher will bear little fruit. Do we priests need to be reminded that the same is true in our own case?

Essential to the process of faith development in the child is that the parents, teacher and priest share their faith with the children. And so the priest goes into the classroom to share his

1

faith with the children. We believe in a God who values and loves each of us individually and personally. He knows the clay from which we are made. He has numbered the hairs on our head, not a big job for some of us! He calls each of us by name. When the priest calls the child by name he/she is reassured of God's personal love and interest. Ideally, in the course of his visit, the priest will make contact with each child, by asking a question or soliciting some response, calling each child by name as he does. In town or city schools where the numbers militate against knowing each child individually, I have found it helpful to have a list of names pinned on the notice-board in the classroom and to use it on each visit to make a roll-call of the class. As well as individual contact with each child present it reminded me to inquire for the absent ones who were sick and also to inquire about a mother or father who was in hospital etc. Through that list I was making a personal contact with the child and with his or her family. By visiting the classroom I was achieving a presence in the home.

As the children benefit from the regular visits of the priest even more so does the teacher. Some priests profess their confidence in their teachers by staying away and letting them get on with the job, 'not bothering them'. Behind this is the idea that the priest's role is that of an overseer. I would hope that most priests today would have a very different idea of their role. Parents, teachers and priests are partners in fostering the faith of the children. We need to work together, to support each other, while recognising our respective roles. It is not the function of the priest to go into the classroom and teach the religion lesson. That's the professional domain of the teacher, who has a manual to follow which is laid out in class lessons with aims and objectives etc. The priest is not a trained teacher and so he feels totally inadequate to this task. If he feels this is what is expected of him in the classroom he will either keep away altogether or feel so ill at ease that his presence merely creates tension. The priest is not expected to do the teacher's work, there's no question of taking over the religion class and allowing the teacher out for a smoke! At the same time what the priest does cannot be at cross purposes with what the teacher is doing. If the teacher is trying to get across an idea of God as a loving and forgiving Father who loves us unconditionally (like the father of the Prodigal Son) and if the priest tries to convey that 'the fear of God is the beginning of wisdom' and the guarantee of right living, the child will end up confused; not knowing whether to love God or to fear him.

The priest needs to be tuned in to what the teacher is doing and his 'chat' to the children needs to harmonise with and, perhaps, fill out what the children have already learned from the teacher. Hence the purpose of this little book. There is a chapter on each year of the programme which gives us the basic thrust or theme of the year's work and shows how this theme is developed in the various units in a particular programme. Knowing this we will be able to tune in to what is happening in the classroom. Rather than giving input the aim should be to solicit feedback from the children:

Tell me about what you are doing.
Tell me about those lovely pictures on the wall.
Read out for me what you have written in your workbook.
Describe for me the picture you have drawn.
Tell me the story you have been doing.
Tell me about Zacchaeus or Jairus, or the woman at the well, or Moses, or Abraham, or Michelangelo, or Oscar Romero, or Mother Teresa, etc.
Tell me more, more, more …

And our reaction should be praise, praise and more praise. Mól an óige agus tiocfaidh siad. (And may I add, 'Mól an muinteoir nó an sagart, agus tiocfaidh sé/sí freisin'.)

Prayer has a special place in the programme. There are prayer services, penance services and para-liturgies and these are special opportunities for us to lead the children to God. The class Mass is an ideal opportunity for priest, teacher and pupils to prepare and celebrate together in a way that achieves 'full and active participation of all people in the Mass' (Council document on the Liturgy). This 'good experience' will leave the children with a positive attitude towards the Mass. Confirmation, First Confession and First Communion are highly significant occasions in the Christian life of the child. The preparation is all-important and calls for the close co-operation of teacher, parents and priest. This book will help the priest to do his part well.

Everyone agrees that this age is a challenging and difficult one in which to lead children to God. We have powerful and well-equipped opponents. To enable us to meet this challenge we are blessed in having the current catechetical programme. With this instrument victory is at least possible. We are deeply indebted to Maura Hyland and those who work with her for this invaluable help to enable us to play our full part in the programme. May we all work together and, with God's help, win this age for Christ.

Fr Michael Deegan

Fr Deegan is parish priest of Ballynacargy, Co. Westmeath, and was formerly diocesan adviser in the diocese of Meath.

INTRODUCTION

The role of the priest who visits the classroom on a regular basis is a vital one in relation to the work of schools in the area of religious education. Teachers often feel inadequate when faced with the burden of religious education. Even the most highly committed often feel that they have received inadequate training and that they are lacking in the theological background that would be helpful. Hence, they ask for a certain level of consistent support from the home and from the parish.

In some instances the level of support and involvement from the home is minimal or non-existent. In such circumstances a teacher who does not experience the active involvement of the local clergy feels that he or she is left to carry this essential part of the Church's mission in isolation.

On a visit to a classroom the priest comes, not in the first place as a teacher, but as a person of faith who is recognised by the children as one having a particular role in the local Church, who seeks to accompany the children on their journey in faith. He comes, therefore, as a friend, as someone who is interested in the children, and who wants to share with the teacher the responsibility of handing on to them the faith of the community, whom he represents.

It is important, in so far as the circumstances of a particular situation allow, to try to build a relationship of friendship and trust with the teachers and with the children. If possible get to know the names of the children, particularly those in the junior infant class and in the classes where children are prepared for the celebration of the sacraments.

If, as a priest, you can visit the school on a fairly regular basis it helps the children to achieve an ease in communication with you that can only be helpful, not merely in terms of your work with them as children but in terms of your subsequent work with them as young adults in the parish.

Sometimes a priest finds it difficult to know exactly what to say to small children. The aim of this book is to provide starting points for discussion and to give the priest an insight into the language that children are familiar with. It provides notes for a number of visits to the classroom each year during the child's time in primary school, from junior infants to sixth class.

PRAYING WITH THE CHILDREN

Religious education seeks to enable the child not only to know about God but to know God. As religious educators we hope to enable them to relate to God as someone who is interested in them and in all their concerns, the things that make them happy and the things that make them sad, someone who knows all their hopes and fears, someone who loves them, forgives them and cares about them. In order to build a relationship communication is necessary. We communicate with God in prayer. So education in prayer is a very important part of religious education.

In the *Children of God* programme particular attention is paid to this aspect of religious education and care is taken right from the beginning, in the first lesson of the junior infant programme, to encourage the teacher to spend some time each week, in the context of the particular lesson of that week, praying with the children. While, each year, we teach the children some of the formal prayers that are in common use, we must keep in mind that teaching children prayers is not necessarily the same thing as teaching children to pray. On the other hand, it is essential that children learn the formal prayer language of the Church, so that they can gradually be initiated into the Church as a worshipping community. They learn to join with their family in prayer in the home. They learn to join with the community in prayer in the church on Sunday. However, as well as ensuring that they are learning to use this formal prayer language we must help them to have an attitude of prayer, to know that God is always listening to them, that God is interested in hearing whatever they want to say about themselves, their needs, their joys, sorrows, hopes or fears. We want them to know that, though there are times when the most appropriate way to pray is through the use of some of the formal prayers they have learned, they can speak to God in whatever language they find easiest to use and that, as in the story of the two men who went into the temple to pray, it is the attitude that is in our heart that is more important than the words we say. In fact sometimes, if our prayer is to be a real expression of those things that are deepest and most meaningful in our lives, the best words are often not those we find on the pages of a book, but those we will find written in our hearts.

In each lesson in the programme there is a prayer service. This is one of the most important parts of the lesson. If the prayer service is left out, the lesson remains incomplete.

The role of the teacher during the prayer service is to pray with the children and to invite them to take part with him or her in prayer. The best time of the week for the prayer service is probably on Friday, when part of the time devoted to the religious education class can be spent in prayer. It is a time when the activity of the classroom takes on a different rhythm, not one of teaching, not one of learning, but one of prayer. On the occasion of a classroom visit the priest can also take up a similar role, that of praying with the children. One way of helping children to pray is to provide opportunities for them to join with adults in prayer. This experience is missing today from the home life of many children. It is all the more important, therefore, that this opportunity be provided in the classroom.

Often, in the classroom, prayers are said first thing in the morning before the real activity of the day begins or last thing in the evening after the work of the day has finished, bags have been packed and the children's attention is focused on the freedom that comes with the ringing of the school bell. Often, too, the prayers are said in a routine fashion, without much thought or preparation either on the part of the teacher or of the pupils.

In the early years the prayer service is very simple. The teacher or priest gives thanks to God for the gift of eyes, people who love us, friends at school, the beauty of nature, as the lesson demands, and the children are invited to imitate the prayer of the adult who is leading the prayer service.

Here there is the opportunity for the priest or teacher to express his or her faith in prayer language and for the children to hear an adult pray.

As the children get older the tone of the prayer service comes from the tone of the lesson in which it is set. Hence sometimes it will be a prayer of thanks for the gifts we have received, sometimes one in praise of the greatness of God, sometimes one of asking for God's help or guidance, sometimes one of sorrow for the wrongs we have done.

The programme suggests some of the following as part of the prayer service: short litanies of praise, thanks or sorrow, depending on the context; a psalm, usually in a translation that is accessible to children; a story from scripture; some of the formal prayers the children have learned; spontaneous prayers.

You may find that there are some things which help create an atmosphere of prayer, for instance you could light a candle; play some soft music; ask the children to sing one of the hymns or songs from the programme.

The programme merely offers suggestions. During your visit to a classroom the prayer service can take whatever form you are most comfortable with yourself and find most helpful for the children.

NEW PRAYER FORMULAS FROM
THE *CHILDREN OF GOD SERIES*

Morning prayer
Father in heaven,
you love me,
you're with me night and day,
I want to love you always,
in all I do and say,
I'll try to please you, Father,
bless me through the day. Amen.

Prayer before meals
Bless us, O God, as we sit together,
bless the food we eat today,
bless the hands that made the food,
bless us, O God. Amen.

Act of faith
O my God, I believe in you,
and in all that your Holy Church teaches,
because you have said it and your word is true.

You are the Christ, the Son of the living God,
you are my Lord and my God.
Lord, I believe, increase my faith.

Act of charity
O my God, I love you with all my heart,
with all my soul, and with all my strength.
Lord, increase our love.
Help us to love one another.

Prayer before the sacrament of penance
God Our Father, help me to remember
the times when I didn't live
as Jesus asked me to.
Help me to be sorry and to try again.

St Patrick's Breastplate
Christ be with me,
Christ be beside me,

Christ be before me,
Christ be behind me,
Christ be at my right hand,
Christ be at my left hand,
Christ be with me everywhere I go,
Christ be my friend for ever and ever. Amen.

Prayer after the Angelus
Lord, fill our hearts with your love,
and as you revealed to us by an angel
the coming of your Son as man,
So lead us through his suffering and death,
to the glory of his Resurrection,
for he lives and reigns with you and the Holy Spirit,
One God, for ever and ever. Amen.

Prayer to the Holy Spirit (adult)
Come, Holy Spirit, fill the hearts of the faithful,
and kindle in them the fire of your love.
Send forth your Spirit, and they shall be created,
and you will renew the face of the earth.
O God who has taught the hearts of the faithful
by the light of the Holy Spirit,
grant us in the same Spirit to be truly wise,
And ever to rejoice in his consolation,
through Jesus Christ Our Lord. Amen.

Prayer to the Holy Spirit (alternative)
Holy Spirit, I want to do what is right.
Help me.
Holy Spirit, I want to live like Jesus.
Guide me.
Holy Spirit, I want to pray like Jesus.
Teach me.

Night prayer
God Our Father, I come to say,
thank you for your love today,
thank you for my family,
And all the friends you give to me
Guard me in the dark of night,
And in the morning send your light. Amen.

Prayer after meals
Thank you, God, for the food we have eaten,
thank you, God, for all our friends,
thank you, God, for everything,
thank you God. Amen.

Act of hope
O my God, I put my hope in you,
because I am sure of your promises.
Deliver us, Lord, from every evil,
and grant us peace in our day,
as we wait in joyful hope
for the coming of our Saviour, Jesus Christ. Amen.

Act of sorrow
O my God, I thank you for loving me,
I am sorry for all my sins,
for not loving others and not loving you.
Help me to live like Jesus and not sin again. Amen.

Prayer after the Sacrament of Penance
God Our Father, thank you for forgiving me.
Help me to love others.
Help me to live as Jesus asked me to.

Prayer to Mary
Mary, Mother of Jesus,
I want to live and love like you,
I want to love the Father,
I want to love like Jesus.
Mother of Jesus, blessed are you,
Mother of Jesus and my mother too,
help me to live like Jesus,
and help me to live like you.

Prayer to the guardian angel
Angel sent by God to guide me;
Be my light and walk beside me;
Be my guardian and protect me;
On the paths of life direct me.

Prayer after Communion
Lord Jesus, I love and adore you,
you're a special friend to me,
Welcome Lord Jesus, O welcome,
thank you for coming to me.

Thank you Lord Jesus, O thank you,
for giving yourself to me,
make me strong to show your love,
wherever I may be.

I'm ready now, Lord Jesus,
to show how much I care,
I'm ready now to give your love,
at home and everywhere.

Be near me, Lord Jesus, I ask you to stay
close by me forever and love me I pray.
Bless all of us children in your loving care,
and bring us to heaven to live with you there.

FORMAL PRAYERS OF THE CHILDREN OF GOD SERIES

TITLE OF PRAYER	Infants, Primary 1&2	First Class, Primary 3	Second Class, Primary 4	Third Class, Primary 5	Fourth Class, Primary 6	Fifth Class, Primary 7	Sixth Class, Post-Primary 1
Sign Of The Cross	Yes	Yes	Yes	Yes	Yes	Yes	Yes
Our Father	Yes	Yes	Yes	Yes	Yes	Yes	Yes
Glory Be To the Father	Yes	Yes	Yes	Yes	Yes	Yes	Yes
Glory To God in The Highest				Yes	Yes	Yes	Yes
The Creed				Yes	Yes	Yes	Yes
Morning Prayer	Yes	Yes	Yes	Yes	Yes	Yes	Yes
Night Prayer	Yes	Yes	Yes	Yes	Yes	Yes	Yes
Grace Before Meals	Yes	Yes	Yes	Yes	Yes	Yes	Yes
Grace After Meals	Yes	Yes	Yes	Yes	Yes	Yes	Yes
St Patrick's Breastplate		Yes	Yes	Yes	Yes	Yes	Yes
Confiteor		Yes	Yes	Yes	Yes	Yes	Yes
Act Of Sorrow		Yes	Yes	Yes	Yes	Yes	Yes
Prayer Before Penance		Yes	Yes	Yes	Yes	Yes	Yes
Prayer After Penance		Yes	Yes	Yes	Yes	Yes	Yes
Prayer Before Communion		Yes	Yes	Yes	Yes	Yes	Yes
Prayer After Communion		Yes	Yes	Yes	Yes	Yes	Yes
The Angelus				Yes	Yes	Yes	Yes
Act of Faith						Yes	Yes
Act Of Hope						Yes	Yes
Act Of Charity						Yes	Yes
Prayer Of St Francis						Yes	Yes

FORMAL PRAYERS OF THE CHILDREN OF GOD SERIES
(continued)

TITLE OF PRAYER	Infants, Primary 1&2	First Class, Primary 3	Second Class, Primary 4	Third Class, Primary 5	Fourth Class, Primary 6	Fifth Class, Primary 7	Sixth Class, Post-Primary 1
Prayer To The Holy Spirit (Adult)						Yes	Yes
Prayer To The Holy Spirit			Yes	Yes	Yes	Yes	Yes
Prayer To The Guardian Angel					Yes	Yes	Yes
Hail Mary	Yes	Yes	Yes	Yes	Yes	Yes	Yes
Prayer To Mary						Yes	Yes
Hail Holy Queen						Yes	Yes
The Magnificat						Yes	Yes
The Memorare						Yes	Yes
Mysteries Of The Rosary				Some	Yes	Yes	Yes
An Phaidir				Yes	Yes	Yes	Yes
Fáilte An Aingil				Yes	Yes	Yes	Yes
Glóir Don Athair				Yes	Yes	Yes	Yes
Paidir Na Maidine						Yes	Yes
Paidir Na hOíche						Yes	Yes
Altú Roimh Bhia						Yes	Yes
Altú Tar Éis Bia						Yes	Yes

JUNIOR INFANTS/PRIMARY 1

Teacher's Book: *The Father Loves You 1*

Pupil's Books: *Catching Sunshine 1* and *2*

Background to the approach in the Junior infant/Primary 1 programme

In this programme we help the children to explore their experience of being alive in the world with other people. We seek to help them come to an awareness of the wonder of life, firstly as they experience it in their own bodies and then as they experience it in the world of nature. We take this as the starting point in our effort to help them become the kind of people who will respect and value all life as sacred. We introduce them to God as the creator, the One who gives life and who sustains it, and we encourage them to respond to God with praise and thanksgiving. We provide opportunities for them to reflect on their lives with others. We help them to become more aware of the love and care which they experience from their parents, family and friends. We help them to become more sensitive to others' needs and to appreciate the joy of doing things with others. We also introduce the children to the feasts of Christmas and Easter.

The themes in this programme are: Me; Autumn; Home; Christmas; Winter; School; Church; Spring; Easter; Other people; Summer. There are suggestions for five visits to the classroom during this year. You can adapt these in any way you wish.

LATE OCTOBER VISIT TO THE CLASSROOM

1.   At this stage of the school year the children are still only beginning to settle into the routine of school. It is important to remember that they have, as yet, only a minimum attention span.

On your first visit of the year you might like to welcome them to the school. You could comment on how they've grown. You could also tell them that you are delighted to see them in school at last.

The children will have completed most of the first two themes in the programme, Me and Autumn, by late October.

2. You could talk with the children about the gift of life. The following might be useful as conversation openers.

3. Ask the children to stay very, very quiet for a moment. You could ask them: What sounds can you hear in the classroom? Outside in the corridor? Outside the window of the classroom? What part of your body are you using to listen to these sounds?

4. Ask the children to think about their eyes. What do you see right now with your eyes? Can anyone see anything bigger? What's the smallest thing you can see? Can anyone see anything smaller?

5. Ask the children if they can remember any story they heard about hands, feet, eyes or ears. They may need to help one another out when retelling a story. Or they may be able to say a poem together.

6. The autumn chart from the *Children of God* kit may be on the wall. They may be able to name Knobbly the Oak and Harry the Hedgehog.

You could ask them: What happens to trees in autumn? What do some animals do in autumn? Would you like to sing the song about Harry the Hedgehog?

7. You could admire their paintings and pictures on the walls. Look at a few of their workbooks. Ask them to tell you about the pictures they have drawn.

8. Before you go you might like to pray with the children. The following may be useful.

Priest:	Before I go we'll spend a few minutes thanking God together for all that he has given us.
	We will start by making the Sign of the Cross together.
All:	In the name of the Father etc.
Priest:	We have hands to do things and to make things.
	We have feet to walk and run and jump.
	We have eyes to see.

We have ears to hear.
We have voices to talk.
We can see the autumn colours.
We can run and play in the countryside.
We can collect leaves.
It's good to be alive.
I'm going to thank God for the gift of life.
God Our Father I'm glad to be alive, thank you.
Let us all thank God together.

All: God Our Father I'm glad to be alive. Thank you.
Glory be to the Father,
and to the Son,
and to the Holy Spirit.

PRE-CHRISTMAS VISIT TO THE CLASSROOM

The children will have completed the theme on Home and will be working on the Christmas theme.

1. You could ask the children if they have any babies at home. Encourage them to talk about the babies. Who looks after the baby? Encourage them to talk about the different jobs that each person does: Mammy, Daddy, themselves; ask them what they do.

There may be a wall chart in the room with photographs of the babies — if so admire it. Look at it and comment on the page in some of their workbooks which deals with this lesson.

2. You could remind them that at Christmas we celebrate the birth of a very special baby. Ask them if they can tell you who that baby was. You could tell them a very simple version of the Christmas story. The teacher may already have told them this story, or perhaps the teacher may not yet have arrived at that point in the programme. Either way this is an appropriate activity, since the children will enjoy listening to the story several times over.

3. Ask them what are they looking forward to at Christmas?

4. Before you go you might like to pray with the children. The following may be useful:

Priest: I'd like to say thanks to God for giving us his Son Jesus.
God Our Father, thank you for sending Jesus into the

17

world on the first Christmas night. Thank you too, for all the happiness and joy of Christmas. Let us all sing the Christmas song 'Jesus was a baby' together.

All sing: 'Jesus was a Baby'
Priest: Let us pray.
All: Glory be to the Father,
and to the Son,
and to the Holy Spirit.

MARCH VISIT TO THE CLASSROOM

After Christmas the children worked on a theme on 'Winter' in which they were helped to become aware of God's care for the earth, for the animals and birds and for all people, during the cold days of winter.

Following this in the theme of 'School' we helped the children to reflect on their lives with others at school. Through the care of the teacher, the children experience the love and care of God, and they discover the signs of God's presence in their lives through the work of the teacher. In their experience of working and playing with other children they begin to discover moral values. In the theme of 'Church' we introduce the children to the church building as God's House.

The following might be useful as conversation starters:

1. Ask the children what they most enjoy doing at school.

2. Comment on their pictures and the art work which is displayed on the walls.

3. You could tell them a story about what it was like when you went to school; where you lived, which school you went to, who your teacher was, the things you most liked to do etc.

4. They may have learned a song which is also a game called 'The Friendly Game'. If the teacher indicates that they have done this, you could ask them to sing it for you.

5. You could pray with them. The following may be helpful:

Priest: Before I go we will spend a few minutes thanking God for all the good things that are part of coming to school. We will begin by making the Sign of the Cross together.
All make the Sign of the Cross.

Priest:　Let us thank God for the people at school.
　　　　God Our Father, thank you for our teacher,
　　　　God Our Father, thank you for all our friends.
　　　　Let us all thank God together.
All:　　God Our Father, thank you for our teacher,
　　　　God Our Father, thank you for our friends.
All:　　Glory be to the Father,
　　　　and to the Son,
　　　　and to the Holy Spirit.

6. You could tell the children the story of Solomon's temple. You might like to look at the version of this story that is included on pp. 92-93 of the teacher's book. Alternatively, you could tell them the story of the presentation in the temple which the children will have heard under the title 'Jesus is brought to God's House'.

7. Ask the children to tell you about the different things they remember seeing in the church.

8. You might like to accompany the teacher and children on a visit to the church. Talk to the children about how the church is a special house decorated in a special way, with very beautiful stained glass windows etc. Talk about the altar, the sanctuary lamp etc.

PRE-EASTER VISIT TO THE CLASSROOM

The children will have completed a theme on 'Spring', in which we help them to become aware of spring as a time of new life. We focus on plants, animals and birds, and by encouraging the children's natural interest and fascination in these we help them to become aware of the wonder of new life.

In the theme on 'Easter' we tell them a simple version of the Easter Story and help them to see Easter as a time for happiness and rejoicing.

The following might be useful as conversation starters:

1. Ask the children to tell you how they would know that spring is here.

2. If the classroom contains any signs of spring, e.g. budding leaves, flowers, plants, pictures, paintings etc., comment on them, ask the children to tell you about them: where they came from, who brought them in etc.

3. Tell the children why you like springtime.

4. The children will have learned a number of stories about animals, plants and birds waking up in springtime. Ask them if they would like to tell you some of these stories. There are stories about Knobbly Oak, Rory the Rabbit and Harry the Hedgehog. They might also sing one of the songs they learned about spring.

5. You could ask them if they know why Easter is a happy time. The programme speaks about Easter as a happy time because Jesus Christ, God's Son is alive and with us. Talk to the children about the different things people do to celebrate at Easter.

6. Tell them a simple version of the Resurrection story; see p. 109, teacher's book.

You might like to pray with the children. You could use the following or any other format which you prefer.

Priest:	Before I go we'll pray together.
	(All make the Sign of the Cross.)
Priest:	God Our Father, thank you for the wonderful things that happen in the countryside in springtime.
	Thank you too for Easter.
	Let us all thank God together.
All:	God Our Father, thank you for the wonderful things that happen in the countryside in springtime.
	Thank you too for Easter.
All:	Glory be to the Father,
	and to the Son,
	and to the Holy Spirit.

SUMMER VISIT TO THE CLASSROOM IN JUNE

The children will have completed a theme on 'Other people'. We help them to appreciate grandparents, the priest and the doctor as people who, in different ways, give them the love and care which they need. Through these people they come to a better understanding of the love and care of God. In the last unit in the programme we help the children, again, to explore God's presence in our lives, through the beauty and joy of summer.

The following might be useful as conversation starting points:

1.   Ask the children to talk about the things they like most about their grannies, about their grandads.

2.   Ask them to talk about times when they need the doctor's help.

3.   Tell them about the things you do as a priest in the parish.

4.   Wish them well at the end of their first year in school. Tell them how you've noticed their growth during the year. Wish them a good holiday. Ask them what they are most looking forward to during the summer.

5.   You could pray with them before you go.

All make the Sign of the Cross.

Priest: At the end of this, your first year in school, we'll thank God for all his blessings and gifts during the year. God Our Father, thank you for all you have given us during this year: for family, for friends, for people who love us, for food, for school where we learn many things, for fun and games, for the beautiful countryside. Thank you for all your love and care.

All: Glory be to the Father
and to the Son,
and to the Holy Spirit,
as it was in the beginning,
is now and ever shall be,
world without end. Amen.

You might like to end by giving the children a simple blessing.

SENIOR INFANTS/PRIMARY 2

Teacher's Book: *The Father Loves You 2*

Pupil's Books: *Catching Sunshine 3* and *4*

Background to the approach in the Senior Infants/Primary 2 programme

In this programme the approach is the same as that of the Junior infants/Primary 1 programme and the same eleven themes are explored, though from a different point of view. There is one additional lesson: 'Jesus grows up'.

LATE SEPTEMBER VISIT TO THE CLASSROOM

The children will have completed the first theme in the programme entitled 'Me', in which they are helped to come to a sense of their own individuality and personal worth. We help them to appreciate their own uniqueness; to become aware that God knows each one of them by name; that God cares for them with a special love and we encourage them to respond to God's love in prayer. We teach them the first lines of the Our Father.

In the second theme of the programme we help the children to become aware of autumn as the time when crops are ripe and seeds are harvested. We help them gradually to come to an awareness of their dependence on the earth, through exploring stories of the farmer's work and the story of a loaf of bread. We help them to experience God's care for us through the fruitfulness of the earth and to come to a sense of our dependence on God.

LATE SEPTEMBER VISIT TO THE CLASSROOM

1. The children have been concentrating on their uniqueness and individuality and so you could take this up as your starting

point for conversation with them. You could get a list of names from the teacher, call each child by name, ask them to stand as their name is called and when they are all standing welcome them back to school for a further year. You might comment on how they've grown during the holidays and tell them that you are looking forward to getting to know them better during the coming year.

2. Ask them if any of them can tell you something about their name, why their parents chose it etc. Tell them your Christian name, and why your parents chose it.

3. You could ask them to talk about autumn, though they will not yet have completed this theme. The following questions may help. What season of the year is this? Name some of the things the farmer does in autumn. What happens in the countryside in autumn?

4. They may have learned the song 'The Farmer Man' — if so this is one of the great favourites in the programme and they will probably be delighted to have an opportunity to sing it for you.

5. Before you go you might like to pray with the children.

All make the Sign of the Cross.

Priest: Each of us has a name.
God knows each of us by name.
Let us give thanks and praise to God for his love and care for each one of us. We are all special in his eyes,
We are different from everybody else in the world;
Let us thank God
For giving us the earth and crops that grow.
For the season of autumn when crops are harvested.
Let us praise God together in the first two lines of the prayer, 'The Our Father':
All: Our Father,
Who art in heaven,
hallowed be thy name.
All make the Sign of Cross.

EARLY DECEMBER VISIT TO THE CLASSROOM

The children will have completed the theme on 'Home', where we help them to appreciate the joy of living with others. We highlight in particular two of the activities that children take part in at home — eating together and praying together. We begin to explore with them the implications of living with others. We encourage them to begin to appreciate the needs of others. At this stage they are probably beginning the Christmas theme. They hear the Christmas story in greater detail than in the Junior Infants programme. They are continuing to learn the Our Father and in the first lesson of the Christmas theme they learn the words of the Hail Mary. They have also been introduced to the Grace before and after meals.

1.   The children may be able to tell you the story of 'Mother hen and her little chicks' which highlights the love and security that children feel at home (p.48 teacher's book). They may be able to sing one of the songs 'Mammy', 'Daddy', or 'Home is happy'.

2.   Ask them to talk about the things that the different people do at home. What are the things that Mammy does at home every day? What does Daddy do? What can you do to help out? What can you do to make others happy at home? Did you ever do anything that caused others to be unhappy at home? (In this context is is important to be sensitive to children who come from broken homes or from one-parent families.)

3.   You could ask them to talk about the times when they pray at home and about the prayers they use.

4.   You could ask them to open their favourite page about 'Home' in their workbooks. Walk around and comment briefly on them.

5.   Before you go you might like to pray with the children.

All make the Sign of the Cross.

Priest:	Today we will say thanks to God again for the people at home who love us.
	Thank you God for Mammy.
All:	Thank you God for Mammy.
Priest:	Thank you God fcr Daddy.
All:	Thank you God for Daddy.
Priest:	Thank you God for my brothers and sisters.
All:	Thank you God for my brothers and sisters.
Priest:	Thank you God for Granny and Grandad.
All:	Thank you God for Granny and Grandad.

Priest:	Thank you God for the food we eat at home.
All:	Thank you God for the food we eat at home.
Priest:	We will say the Our Father together.
All:	Our Father ...

All make the Sign of Cross.

MID-FEBRUARY VISIT TO THE CLASSROOM

In this programme there is a lesson entitled 'Jesus Grows Up' which helps the children come to know Jesus as someone who was once a child, who grew and learned, who played with other children, who helped Mary and who watched the shepherds and fishermen at their work.

1. In this visit you could simply talk to the children about Jesus as a boy. He lived with Mary and Joseph; talk about what they did all day.
— Mary made bread, fetched water from the village well etc.
— Joseph worked in the carpenter's shop.
Talk about the warm weather in the country where Jesus lived.

2. Ask them to talk about the two pages in their workbooks which deal with this lesson.

3. They may know the song 'When Jesus was a boy'. If so, ask them to sing it.

4. Before you go you might like to pray with them.

All make the Sign of the Cross.

Priest:	Today we will pray together to thank God for Jesus.
All:	'Thank you God for Jesus',
	is the prayer we say.
	'Thank you, God, for Jesus,
	thank you every day'.
Priest:	We will finish by praising God together in one of the prayers that Jesus learned when he was a boy.
All:	Holy are you,
	holy is your name,
	O Lord Our God.

All make the Sign of the Cross.

APRIL/PRE-EASTER VISIT TO THE CLASSROOM

The children will have completed themes on 'School' and 'Other people' and will now be working on the theme 'Spring', which prepares them to think about new life in the context of Easter.

They will have been focusing on the love and care which they experience from others at school and in the neighbourhood. They will also have been encouraged to become more sensitive to the needs of others. In the theme on spring we focus on the natural interest that the children have in nature and we encourage them to wonder at the re-awakening of the world of nature in spring-time. In this way we help them to become more aware of the action of God in the world.

1.   You could tell the chldren about the things which you like most in springtime. Tell them what you noticed on your way to the school today.

2.   Ask them to talk about what they like best about springtime.

3.   If there are plants growing in the classroom or pictures showing spring scenes comment on these.

4.   Ask them to sing one of the songs they have learned about springtime.

5.   You could tell them a story about a shepherd caring for his sheep (see p.101 teacher's book). Tell them that God is sometimes called the Good Shepherd. When we see a shepherd taking care of sheep we are reminded of God's care for us.

6.   If you wish to pray with them before you leave, you might like to use this litany.

All make the Sign of the Cross.

Priest: Spring is a time of new life.
Let us thank God Our Father for new life in spring.
All: God Our Father, thank you for new life in spring.
Priest: Let us thank God Our Father for new green leaves in spring.
All: God Our Father, thank you for new green leaves in spring.
Priest: Let us thank God Our Father for daffodils, primroses and snowdrops.

All:	God Our Father, thank you for daffodils, primroses and snowdrops.
Priest:	Let us thank God Our Father for baby lambs.
All:	God Our Father, thank you for baby lambs.
Priest:	Let us thank God Our Father for baby birds in springtime.
All:	God Our Father, thank you for baby birds in springtime.
Priest:	Let us thank God Our Father for all the love and care he shows in springtime.
All:	God Our Father, thank you for all your love and care in springtime.
Priest:	Let us pray together in the words of the Our Father:
All:	Our Father...

SUMMER VISIT TO THE CLASSROOM

The children have completed a unit entitled 'Church'. The two lessons in this unit are called 'Sunday Mass' and 'The priest'.

The following are some examples of how you might engage the children in conversation around these topics.

1. Remind the children that we go to Mass on Sunday to thank God Our Father for all his love and care.

Ask them to tell you what they remember about being at Mass on Sunday.

Ask them what they like best about being at Mass on Sunday.

2. Perhaps, if it is convenient, you might accompany the children on a visit to the local church. During the visit you might spend some time praying with the children. You could also help them to become aware of the different aspects of the church building: the stained glass windows; the altar; the tabernacle; the sanctuary lamp; the holy water font at the door etc.

If this is not appropriate you could look at the children's pictures of the church in their workbooks. Ask them to tell you what they remember about the church. Ask them to tell you what they remember having seen on the altar during Mass on Sunday.

3. Moving on to the lesson on the priest you might like to tell them about yourself: Your Christian name; where you lived as a young boy; what life was like when you were growing up; what games you played; where you went to school. You could also talk about your work in the parish as a priest: celebrating

the sacraments with the people; visiting people in their homes, especially those who are sick or lonely; tell them that coming into the school to see them is a very special part of your work.

4. You might like to pray with the children before you go.

All make the Sign of the Cross.

Priest: As we come near the end of the school year we will spend a few moments thanking God Our Father for all his care and his blessings during this year:
For friends we have made
For the fun and games we have enjoyed
For all we have learned in school
For our mammies and daddies who look after us at home
For the teacher who looks after us in school
For the countryside around us
(Encourage the children to mention some of the things which they would like to thank God for.)
Let us all thank God together in the words of the Glory be to the Father:

All: Glory be to the Father ...

FIRST CLASS/PRIMARY 3

Teacher's Book: *Show us the Father*

Pupil's Book: *Come and See*

Background to the approach in the First Class/Primary 3 programme

The title of this programme is taken from St John's Gospel (14:9) in which the apostle Philip says to Jesus: 'Show us the Father'. The title of the pupil's book recalls Jesus' invitation to two of John's disciples: 'Come and see.' In this programme we help the children to come to know God, firstly through an exploration of the gift of life which they experience in their own bodies, in their relationships with others and in the world around them and, secondly, as he is shown to us by Jesus. Jesus showed us in his life and in the way he treated others the love, care and forgiveness of God. He also showed us how to respond to God's goodness by his life and by his death, which was his final response to the Father. God the Father raised Jesus to new life — we help the children to reflect on the mystery of the resurrection. The children, in the course of this year's programme prepare to celebrate, for the first time, the forgiveness of God in the Sacrament of Reconciliation and to receive the risen Jesus as the Bread of Life in First Holy Communion. We introduce the children to the Holy Spirit who helped the early Christian communities to live as followers of the risen Jesus and who continues to help us today.

In this programme notes will be provided for a visit to the classroom at the end of each unit. You can, however, adapt these to suit your own circumstances.

UNIT 1
GOD OUR FATHER GIVES US THE GIFT OF LIFE

In this unit we explore again some of the ideas contained in the infant programmes but at a slightly deeper level. We help the children to reflect again on their ability to see, hear, make, speak and love. We help them to come to an awareness of the fact that having eyes to see and ears to hear etc. is a gift that we have been given, one that we didn't earn or deserve and that, therefore, it is right that we be truly thankful and that we use this gift creatively in our lives and in co-operation with the other people around us. The lessons move from the experiential level where the children are helped, through reflection on their own experience of life, to come to know that it is good to be able to see, to be able to hear, to have the ability to work, run, jump and play etc., to the prayer service at the end of each lesson where the children are invited to give praise and thanks to God, the creator, the one who gives life and who sustains life. We hope that, through the work that will have been done at the experiential and reflective level, the children will have come to the awareness that it is indeed 'right to give him thanks and praise'.

The lessons in this unit are:

The gift of sight
The gift of hearing
The gift of making
The gift of speech
The gift of love

CLASSROOM VISITATION LINKED TO UNIT 1

1.   You might like, if this is your first visit of the year, to welcome the children back after the summer holidays. Once again, tell them how you have noticed the way in which they have grown during the holidays. Remind them that this is a very special year when they will be preparing for First Confession and First Holy Communion. Assure them that you and their teacher will help them in any way you can during this year.

2.   You could encourage the children to think about the way in which their lives are enriched through having eyes, ears, hands etc. Ask them to open their books at p.4. Read with them the poem 'The Blind Man'.
   You could encourage them to talk about what they would miss most if they were unable to see. Encourage them to talk about situations where they would have to find a different way of dealing with reality, e.g. How would you find your way to the classroom? How could you read, or write? How could you tie your shoe? etc.

3. You could encourage the children to talk about the different things they can do with their hands. You could ask them to think about the kind, gentle things they can do or, on the other hand, they could think about the unkind or cruel things they do. You could carry on a similar conversation with the children about having a voice, feet, ears.

4. The last lesson in the unit is entitled 'I can love'. On p. 57 of the teacher's book you will find the poem 'The Present'. You could read this poem for the children. They may know some of it and will possibly be able to join in with you as you read.

The one gift that we all have is the gift of being able to love. The one gift that we can all give to others is the gift of our love. It is the most important thing that we have to give other people. Encourage the children to talk about ways in which they give their love to other people, to their parents, to their brothers and sisters, to their teacher and friends in school etc.

5. Before you leave you may like to spend some minutes praying with the children.

Priest: Let us spend a few minutes giving thanks and praise to God for all that he has given us.
         All make the Sign of the Cross.
Priest: We'll say the Our Father together and you can show me how you can use your hands as well as your voice to praise God in the Our Father.
All: Our Father...
Priest: Let us read together the prayer of thanks on p.13 of your books.

N.B. You might like to split the class in two halves, one half saying the prayer, the other the response.

Priest: Would anybody like to make their own prayer of thanks to God?

(You could start by saying a prayer yourself, e.g. 'Thank you God for my feet, I use them every day when I walk around the parish, when I visit houses, when I visit the school, when I do my shopping. I'm glad that I have feet.' Encourage the children to respond, as in their book, 'Thank you God Our Father. You are good to us.')

Final prayer : Glory be to the Father...

VISIT AT THE END OF UNIT 2

CLASSROOM VISITATION LINKED TO UNIT 2

God Our Father gives us the gift of life with others. In Unit 2 we help the children to become more aware of the ways in which their lives are enriched by the other people with whom they live and those whom they meet in the neighbourhood. We help them to appreciate the efforts other people make on their behalf and we encourage them to respond by being prepared, at times, to put other people's needs bfore their own. This effort to move out of the egocentric world of the young child is an important step towards moral development. We help them to begin to be aware of the choices they make in terms of how they behave with others. We help them to take perspective — to assess how their choice of behaviour is affecting the lives of those around them.

We help them in a particular way to reflect on the experience of sharing food with others. Eating keeps us alive and those who give us food give us life. Eating with others demands an attitude of sharing and of being prepared to be sensitive to the needs of others. We help them to think of the different contexts and occasions when we share food with others — a family meal, a celebration meal, a meal with one other person. Eating and drinking with others provides a context for sharing not just food, but for being present to others in such a way that we share ourselves with them. At these times too, we communicate with people, we build up friendships. This is an important part of the preparation which will help children to understand the significance of sharing the Bread of Life in Holy Communion.

The lessons in this unit are:

We live in a family
We eat together
We play together
Other people help us

1. It might be a good idea to start by telling the children a story which will prompt discussion on the different choices we make and the ways in which these choices affect others. The following story is a possibility but you may prefer to use your own.

Nuala and Sean had asked their Mammy if it was all right to bring home their friends Peter and Una to play after school. Mammy had agreed and so the four children arrived home together. Mammy gave them each a glass of milk and a sandwich and they went upstairs to play in the girls' bedroom. 'Be careful that you don't touch any of Sarah's things', warned Mammy as they disappeared up the stairs. Sarah was Nuala and Sean's older sister and they knew how annoyed she would be so they agreed to be very careful.

They played houses with Nuala's dolls and teddy. Sean and Una pretended to be the parents in one family and Nuala and Peter pretended to be the parents in the other family. They visited each others' houses and had tea. They took their children, the doll and the teddy, to school and they went together to do their shopping. When they got tired of that game Sean brought in his jigsaw puzzle and they spent a lot of time trying to put the pieces together properly. Soon they heard the horn of a car blowing outside. Peter and Una's mother had come to collect them. The children waved goodbye to their friends from the upstairs window. Then they turned and looked at the room. There were things thrown everywhere. Toy cups and saucers which they had used for the tea, covers and sheets from the doll's pram, books which they had left on the floor so that they could make a space for the jigsaw puzzle. The place was so cluttered that it was difficult to walk from one side of the room to the other.

The children stood looking at the mess. 'What'll we do now?' asked Nuala, 'Will we tidy up this mess or will we leave it here and go out to play?'

The following talking points might prove useful as discussion starters.

What would be the easiest thing for the children to do? Why? How would it affect Mammy if they left the room in a mess? Does anything like this ever happen in your home? Does anything like this ever happen in the classroom? Talk about a time when you did something which didn't make things easy for your Mammy or for the teacher. Talk about a time when you did something which did make things easy for other people.

2. Tell them about a time when you had to make a difficult choice in order to help somebody out. Tell them of a time when

you knew someone else made a difficult choice in order to help you out.

3. Ask them to talk about some of the people whose work helps them and others in the neighbourhood, e.g. the postman, the doctor etc.

4. In this unit the children are helped to reflect upon their experience of playing games with other children. Ask them to talk about some of the things which happen when they play games with other children. Through reflecting on this experience they can become more aware of the values of co-operation, team-work, common effort, fair play, trust etc. Help them to think about the kinds of behaviour that make a game go well and the kinds of behaviour that make a game go badly.

5. Ask them if they can tell you the story of Tom the Woodcutter.

Encourage them to talk about the three different kinds of meal that take place in this story: the simple meal shared by two people in the forest, the family meal and the banquet in the king's palace. They may need to help one another out in telling the story. You will find the story on p.69 of the teacher's book. Ask them to talk about times when they have meals similar to those mentioned in the story — lunch-time in school, family meals, a wedding, christening etc. Encourage them to talk about all that happens when people share food together.

UNIT 3
JESUS SHOWS US THE FATHER

God has given us many gifts: the gift of life; the ability to explore and enjoy the world; family, friends and many other people to love and care for us. God's greatest gift to us, the greatest sign of his love for us, is his son Jesus Christ.

Jesus is the 'image of the unseen God' *(Col 1:15)*. Jesus shows us the true face of God. In his own life, in his deeds, in his attitudes towards people, Jesus shows us who God is and what he is like: loving, concerned, compassionate, forgiving, accepting. Jesus told them that the Father loved them and he showed them what that meant in his own life when he loved not only those whom everybody loved but also those whom nobody loved. He told them that the Father forgave them and in his own life he forgave not only those who appeared to deserve forgiveness but also those who appeared not even to be worthy of forgiveness. In his life with people they saw in action the love, concern, compassion, forgiveness, acceptance of the father in action. When Philip said 'Lord, let us see the Father', Jesus replied, 'To have seen me is to have seen the Father'.

In this unit we help the children to come to know Jesus through introducing them to some of the events in the life of Jesus. We want them to come to know Jesus as someone truly human who, as he grew, learned to walk, to talk, to read, to write, to play. We introduce the children to some stories from the life of Jesus which show how he loved and cared for people. We help them too to become aware of the unique relationship that Jesus had with the Father, through helping them to become aware of the way in which he related to the Father in prayer.

The lessons in this unit are:

Jesus grows up in Nazareth
Jesus has good news
Jesus had many friends
Jesus loved children
Mary the Mother of Jesus
Jesus Christ, the Son of God, is born in Bethlehem
Jesus teaches us to pray to God Our Father

CLASSROOM VISITATION LINKED TO UNIT 3

You might like to pay a special visit to the classroom for Christmas. Since this unit includes the Christmas lessons there is a suggestion for a visit that focuses particularly on Christmas and for another visit that focuses on the remainder of the unit. Alternatively, you may like to combine these.

You can use as many as you like of the following suggestions:

1. Ask the children to talk about some of the things that might have happened in the life of Jesus when he was a boy, e.g. What were the things he might have seen happening in the countryside where he lived? What were some of the things that he may have done with his friends? The children might be able to sing a song about Jesus as a child: 'Jesus was a happy child' or 'When Jesus was a boy'.

2. Ask them if they heard any good news lately. They may talk about a circus coming to town, or their favourite programmes returning on TV, or getting a free day from school. Tell them about some good news you heard. Ask them if Jesus had any good news for the people. Encourage them to talk about the good news that Jesus had.

3. Ask them to talk about some of the people who were friends of Jesus. Those mentioned in the programme are Mary, Martha and Lazarus; the old woman who lived in Peter's house; the twelve apostles. They may be able to tell the story of Jesus in the house of Mary, Martha and Lazarus, or of Jesus healing the woman in Peter's house.

4. A central place in this unit is given to a lesson on the story of Jesus and the children. This is a story that appeals in a very particular way to these children because they can identify with the children in the story. Encourage them to tell you the story. Encourage them to help one another out if necessary. Encourage them to talk about how the children felt at different times in the story, e.g. how they felt when they were setting out on the journey; how they felt when it seemed that they would have to go away without meeting Jesus; how they felt when they actually met Jesus. You could ask them to imagine that Jesus spoke to them individually. What did he say to them? What did they say to Jesus? How did they feel as they left to return home? What did they say to the people at home about their meeting with Jesus? Ask them to sing the song 'Jesus Loves Children'. You'll find this on p.100 of the teacher's book.

5. Ask the children to tell you the story of the day Jesus taught his friends to pray.

6. Before you leave you might like to pray with the children. This is an example of what you might do.

> All make the Sign of the Cross.

Priest: Let us spend a few minutes thinking about Jesus, about some of the things which he did and said. Let us thank God for sending Jesus to teach us how to love. We think of the good news Jesus had for the people. 'God loves you', he said. That news is still true for us today, God loves us. Let us thank God for Jesus.

All: Thank you God for Jesus.

Priest:	Let us think about the time he spent with his special friends; with Mary, Martha and Lazarus; with the apostles; with those who were sick. Let us thank God for Jesus.
All:	Thank you God for Jesus.
Priest:	Let us think of the day when Jesus met with the children. He had time for them. He blessed them. He talked to them. He listened to them. Let us thank God for Jesus.
All:	Thank you God for Jesus.
Priest:	We'll finish by praying together the prayer which gives thanks to God for Jesus.
All:	'Thank you God for Jesus', is the prayer we say. 'Thank you God for Jesus. Thank you every day'.

Alternatively, you could use the prayer service on pp. 100-101 of the teacher's book. This prayer service is based on the story of Jesus and the children. The person who is leading the prayer service simply retells the story slowly and meditatively, helping the children to reflect on the story as they do. It is a simple way of introducing the children to silent prayer. They are being asked to spend some time in silent reflection. But as they do, they are helped to do this by the leader who suggests a line of reflection which is based on the story for them to follow.

CHRISTMAS VISIT

The two lessons which are directly related to Christmas in this programme are 'Mary the mother of Jesus' and 'Jesus Christ, the Son of God, is born in Bethlehem'.

1. You could ask the children to tell you what they know about Mary. You could also talk to them about Mary. You could tell them why you think of Mary as someone special. You could ask them to sing for you one of the songs they have learned in honour of Mary.

2. The story of the birth of Jesus at Christmas is one that the children never tire of. You could tell this story to the children or invite them to tell you the story. Ask them to talk about the many ways in which they are preparing for Christmas at home and in school. Ask them to talk about the reason why we put

so much effort into our preparations for Christmas. Talk to them about why Christmas is a special time for you. The children have probably prepared a Christmas play. If so, they would love to present it for you before you go.

UNIT 4

In this unit we concentrate on the children's moral development. It is a lead-up to the Sacrament of Reconciliation. We help them to reflect again on their own lives in the light of the call of Jesus to 'love one another'. We help them to become aware that sometimes they act in ways that do not show the others who are touched by their actions that they love them; they fail to take into account the effect their actions may have on others, they are selfish and think only of themselves. We also help them to become aware of the fact that sometimes they act out of care and consideration for others. At these times their actions show others that they love and care for them: they put the needs of others before their own needs; they are unselfish. We help them to be aware of the love and forgiveness of God which is always available to us when we fail. Jesus showed us the forgiveness of God in his own dealings with those who had sinned. This year we concentrate on the story of Jesus and Zacchaeus. Jesus reached out to Zacchaeus while he was still locked in his own sinfulness. In the Sacrament of Reconciliation they have an opportunity to articulate their own sinfulness and to experience the love and forgiveness of the Father. The programme recommends that the child's first celebration of the Sacrament of Reconciliation be according to Rite II. In preparing them for the sacrament we try to ensure that their celebration of the sacrament will be linked to their experience of life and so we encourage them to tell the priest a story of a time when they failed to love. This helps the children to take part in the sacrament in a way that is linked to their concrete life experience. It is important to impress upon the children during a visit before their celebration of the Sacrament of Reconciliation that they can approach the priest without fear and that you are there to help them.

1.   You could ask the children if they remember the stories they heard (from the programme) about times when children acted with love and care for one another. There is a story about sharing apples and one about a bottle of bubbles. You will find

these on pp. 117 and 118 of the teacher's book. They are very short and take only a few moments to read. Ask them to tell stories of times when they acted out of love and care for others. Tell them a story about a time when you did something which took another's feelings into consideration, though it was not the easiest thing to do at the time.

2. Ask the children if they can remember the stories they heard from the programme about times when children were selfish, the story about the game of ball or the one about the time when Daddy was sick. Ask them to talk about the way the children acted in these stories. Encourage them to tell stories of times when they were selfish. Tell them a story about a time when you were selfish.

3. Ask them to tell you the story of Zacchaeus. Discuss the story with them. The following questions may help the discussion: What kind of person was Zacchaeus? Why do you think nobody liked him? How do you think Zacchaeus felt that day as he stood alone in the crowd? What did Jesus do? What did the people think of the way in which Jesus treated Zacchaeus? What did Jesus say to Zacchaeus? How did Zacchaeus feel? What did Zacchaeus say? Ask them if they can sing the song about Zacchaeus.

4. Ask them if they can remember the story about Mary 'Down at the Mill'. This is a story about a girl who disobeys her parents, realises she has done wrong, and says sorry. Her parents forgive her. It explores in a simple way the process of reconciliation. Tell the children a story about a time when you had to say sorry for something you had done which you realised was wrong and were forgiven. Tell them a story about a time when someone said sorry to you and you forgave them.

5. Talk to the children about the forgiveness of the Father in the Sacrament of Reconciliation. Assure them that God is always ready, always waiting to forgive us for the wrong things we have done. He waits until we realise that we have done wrong, admit it and say sorry. Assure them that there is no need to be nervous or afraid, that even if they forget what to say when they come for the first time to celebrate the Sacrament of Reconciliation, that you will be there to help them.

6. Before you go you might like to take part in a short penance service with the children. You will find an appropriate

one on pp. 136-7 of the teacher's book. Alternatively, you might like to help the children to reflect further, in prayer or on the story of Zacchaeus as in the prayer service on pp. 127-8 of the teacher's book. You could also substitute any format you prefer if it is in keeping with the language and ideas that the children are familiar with.

UNIT 5

This unit prepares the children for their First Communion by helping them to come to a simple understanding of the structure and meaning of the Mass. We help them to identify some of the parts of the Mass and to relate these to the actions of Jesus and to their own life experience. We help them to come to an awareness of the real presence of the risen Jesus at Mass. We help them to be able to take part more fully in the Mass. We relate back to the material they have already covered in the earlier part of the programme, in Unit 2, on shared meals. For Jesus, as for all Jews, meals were important and involved more than simply satisfying one's hunger. A shared meal was a shared life. Every meal was a religious meal — a sign that they acknowledged their dependence on one another and on God.

The Last Supper took place at a Passover meal when every Jewish family remembered their deliverance from Egypt under Moses. At this meal Jesus was conscious of his own impending death and he gave himself to his disciples in bread and wine. What he had done, he asked his disciples to do in his memory and he told them that in doing it he would be with them. We help the children to appreciate that in gathering together to celebrate the presence of the risen Jesus at Mass we are also accepting the challenge to try to live as he lived. The following diagram provides a summary of the material covered.

APPROACH		
Action of Jesus	Action of the people	Action of the risen Jesus
Jesus celebrated with many people, e.g. Martha, Mary, Lazarus, at the Last Supper.	We celebrate together.	The risen Jesus is with us when we celebrate at Mass.

APPROACH

Action of Jesus	Action of the people	Action of the risen Jesus
Jesus gathered people together, e.g. fishermen and tax-collectors were among his apostles.	We come together at Mass.	The risen Jesus is with us when we gather for Mass.
Jesus told the people good news. This good news helped people to change their lives.	We listen to the words of Jesus.	The risen Jesus speaks to us at Mass.
Jesus reminded the people that God loved them. He made his love real for them by dying on the cross to show us how he loved the Father and to share his life and his love with them.	At Mass we remember that Jesus loved us so much that he died for us, and we give thanks.	The risen Jesus is present with all the love he had for us when he died on the cross and rose to new life.
Jesus showed the people the forgiveness of God our Father. He forgave Zacchaeus etc.	At Mass we celebrate the forgiveness of God our Father.	At Mass the risen Jesus gives us the forgiveness of the Father.
Jesus gave himself to God Our Father and to all people.	At Mass we share the bread of life.	At Mass the risen Jesus gives us the bread of life which is himself.
After the Last Supper, the apostles remembered his	We go from Mass to live as Jesus asked us to live.	The risen Jesus in the Eucharist offers his life, death and

41

APPROACH		
Action of Jesus	**Action of the people**	**Action of the risen Jesus**
life, death and resurrection. They remembered his words, 'Do this in memory of me'. They celebrated the Eucharist as he had told them to do. They went out to live as he had asked them to live. They remembered that it was Jesus who taught us what love means by giving his life for us.		resurrection to the Father for us. He asks us to go from Mass to live lives of love for God our Father and for others.

CLASSROOM VISITATION AT THE BEGINNING OF UNIT 5

1.   Encourage the children to talk about the various celebrations that they have taken part in at home or at school — birthday parties, Christmas, outings, nature walks etc. The following may help to start the discussion.
What was the best celebration you ever took part in?
How do people usually show that they are happy at a celebration?
Tell them about a celebration you remember — perhaps your ordination. Talk about what was special, how it was celebrated etc.
   Help the children to appreciate that this is a time of celebration for all of them. They are preparing to receive for the first time the Bread of Life in Holy Communion. On p. 157 of the teacher's book there is a prayerful celebration to mark the beginning of the children's time of preparation for Holy Communion. You might like to take part in this celebration with the teacher and children. During the prayer service each child's name is mentioned and God's blessing is asked for each one.

FURTHER VISIT DURING UNIT 5 BEFORE FIRST COMMUNION

1. When we teach six-year-olds about the Mass we must remember that we celebrate the Eucharist in a highly ritualistic way, using set language, actions, symbols and gestures. Much of the language that is used and the concepts that this language tries to convey are totally outside the six-year-old's capacity for understanding.

It is good to talk to the children simply about parts of the Mass that they will recognise and link with something that they already understand, e.g. we stand at the Gospel; we listen; the Gospel is the word of Jesus. Ask them to recall some of the things they know Jesus said. Very often, though children learn in school that when they stand for the Gospel they hear the word of Jesus, their experience of Sunday Mass is that, even if they try very hard to listen, they cannot actually hear because the language is too difficult for them. It is important, therefore, to make sure that on the occasion of their First Communion they have the experience of listening to a Gospel that they can actually recognise and hear.

2. At Mass we remember what Jesus did at the Last Supper. We remember his death on the cross. We remember his great love for the Father and for us.

We hear the story of the Last Supper. During the Eucharistic Prayer you could ask the children to tell the story of the Last Supper. At Mass the priest does what Jesus did at the Last Supper. He takes bread, blesses it, breaks it, shares it. He says, 'Take this all of you and eat it. This is my body which will be given for you.' He takes the chalice. He blesses it and says, 'Take this all of you and drink. This is my blood, which will be given for you.' The bread and wine are now the body and blood of Jesus. When we eat this bread in Holy Communion we eat the Bread of Life. Talk to the children about what you do at Mass.

3. Remind the children of their celebration of God's forgiveness in the Sacrament of Reconciliation. Ask them to recall that experience. What do they remember about it?
What did they like most about it?
Ask them if they know that we also celebrate the forgiveness of God the Father at Mass.

Ask if they can remember the words we say at these times: 'Lord have mercy.' 'Christ have mercy.' 'Lamb of God ...'.

Encourage them to talk about the sign of peace. This is an important point for children because they can actually be involved in making the gesture.

Something that they can do is likely to have a greater impact on them than something that they simply listen to. You could ask them:

When do you shake hands with someone?

What does it mean when we shake hands at Mass?

4.   Tell the children the story of the 'Loaves and Fishes'. At the end of the story Jesus says he will give himself as the Bread of Life. In Holy Communion the Risen Jesus gives himself to us as the Bread of Life.

Ask the children if they can remember any story they heard about bread or about meals.

Why do we eat?

What does food do for our bodies?

5.   At the end of Mass the priest says 'Go in peace to love and serve the Lord'.

Ask the children if they can tell you what they would do if they wanted to 'love and serve the Lord' at home, at school, at play.

6.   Ask the children to sing some of the hymns they have learned in this unit.

'We come to you Lord Jesus'
'Céad Míle Fáilte'
'Lord Jesus Welcome'
'Go now in Peace' etc.

UNIT 6
THE LORD JESUS IS ALIVE

Depending on the timing of First Communion and of Easter, this unit may well be completed before Unit 5 in a particular school year. In this unit we introduce the children to the Last Supper, death and resurrection of Jesus.

VISIT AT EASTER

1.   You could ask the children if they can remember the stories they have heard of times when Jesus shared meals with people. They will have heard of the visit to Mary, Martha and Lazarus and the story of Zacchaeus. Ask them to tell you anything they know about the special Jewish meal, the Passover. Tell them or ask them to tell you the story of the Last Supper. Emphasise with them Jesus' commandment of love: 'Love one another as I have loved you', and his promise to send the Holy Spirit.

2.   Ask the children to tell you the story of the crucifixion. Ask them if they can name the people in the story. Encourage them to talk about how Jesus showed love to these people.

3.   Tell the children the story of the resurrection. The story used in this year's programme is the story of Jesus meeting Mary Magdalene in the garden. Talk to them about the Paschal Candle which they will see in the Church on Easter Sunday morning. Refer to the poster of the Paschal Candle which will probably be displayed in the classroom.

4.   You might like to pray with the children before you leave. If the teacher has a candle in the classroom you could use it during the prayer.

All make the Sign of the Cross.

Priest: Let us spend a few moments thinking of the many ways in which Jesus showed his love for us. We will thank God for sending Jesus.
We think of the night of the Last Supper when he shared a meal for the last time with his friends. He promised to be with them always. He is with us today. We pray together.

All: Christ has died,
Christ is risen,
Christ will come again.

Priest: We think of his death on the cross. We remember his forgiveness even for those who crucified him. We pray together.

All: Christ has died,
Christ is risen,
Christ will come again.

Priest:	We think of his resurrection from the dead. We can imagine how delighted his friends were to have him with them again. The risen Jesus is with us too. We light a special candle on Easter Sunday to remind us that he is with us. We will light this candle now to remind us that he is with us.
	We pray together.
All:	Christ has died, Christ is risen, Christ will come again.

UNIT 7
THE HOLY SPIRIT

In this unit we help the children to come to know that they are all children of God, and that through Baptism they became part of God's family. We introduce them to the story of Pentecost. This unit and the year's programme concludes with a lesson which emphasises the importance of prayer.

VISIT TOWARDS THE END OF THE SCHOOL YEAR

1.   Ask the children if they have ever been at the Baptism of a younger brother or sister. Encourage them to talk about the preparations at home. Ask them what happens. The aspects of Baptism that have been emphasised this year are the pouring of water and the Sign of the Cross.

2.   Tell them the story of Pentecost. Encourage them to talk about how the Holy Spirit helped the apostles.

3.   Tell them about the prayers you like to pray and talk about why you like them.

4.   Wish them well during the summer holidays.

5.   Before you go you might like to pray with the children.

   All make the Sign of the Cross.

Priest:	As we come to the end of the school year we give thanks for all the good times we had together during the year. For all we learned,

for all the fun we had,
for the friends we made,
we thank God together.

All: Glory be to the Father,
and to the Son,
and to the Holy Spirit,
as it was in the beginning,
is now,
and ever shall be,
world without end. Amen.

Priest: We give thanks too for all we have come to know about God and about Jesus. We ask the Holy Spirit to help us to learn more and more.

All: Holy Spirit, I want to do what is right,
Help me.
Holy Spirit, I want to live like Jesus,
Guide me.
Holy Spirit, I want to pray like Jesus,
Teach me.

Priest: We ask God to be with us during the summer holidays. Bless us and keep us safe. Bless our families too and all those we will meet during the holidays.

All: Glory be to the Father,
and to the Son,
and to the Holy Spirit,
as it was in the beginning,
is now,
and ever shall be,
world without end. Amen.

SECOND CLASS/PRIMARY 4

Teacher's Book: *You Are My Friends*

Pupil's Book: *My Friends*

Background to the approach in the Second Class/Primary 4 programme

The theme for this year's programme is 'Friendship'. We help the children to reflect on their experience of friendship so that they can come to a deeper understanding of the qualities of human relationships. From this we help them to come to a deeper understanding of their relationship with God. We explore with them the way in which Jesus related in friendship to the children, the apostles, the sick, the sinners. In the love and care of Jesus we can see most clearly the love and care of God for us and for all people. In the life and actions of Jesus we see how we should respond in our own lives to the love and care of God.

UNIT 1
GOD OUR FATHER GIVES US THE JOY OF HAVING FRIENDS

In this unit we help the children to reflect on their experience of life with others at home and at school. We help them to become aware of the fact that our relationships with others help us to grow. We help them to see that we are all interdependent and to appreciate the values of co-operation, sharing, communication, trust, love, happiness. God is the source of all happiness, friendship, love. He has given us the capacity for friendship and for love. He wants us to be happy with him and with others. He has also given us the world to explore and enjoy with others. He invites us to co-operate with him and with others in developing and improving it. We help the children to see that they are called to respond to God for all these signs of goodness and care. The exploration of the children's experience of living

48

with others is also helpful towards their growth in moral development. We help them to see that just as other people contribute to their happiness or unhappiness, they, too, can make others happy or unhappy.

The lessons in this unit are:

We are friends at home
I have friends at school
Friends help one another
Friends enjoy God's world together
Friends eat together

CLASSROOM VISITATION LINKED WITH UNIT 1

1.   If this is your first visit of the year welcome the children back after the summer holidays etc.

2.   Tell the children about a particular friend that you have — why this person is important for you, what you do together, how this person helps you in your life, how you help the other person, what you like most about them etc.

3.   Encourage the children to talk about having friends. You could ask questions such as: Who are your friends? Who is your best friend? Why are you glad to have friends? Can you remember any stories from the programme which talk about how good it is to have friends? Tell me a story about a time in your life when one of your friends helped you. Tell me a story about a time when you helped one of your friends.

4.   You might like to look at the story 'The Seaside' on p. 48 of the teacher's book. It's a simple story based on an experience that is fairly commonplace in a child's life which emphasises the values of sharing, co-operation and the importance of recognising another's gifts and talents. Ask the children to tell you the story, or you could tell them the story, or a similar one which you could make up yourself. Encourage the children to discuss the behaviour of those in the story. Ask them if they can tell you about similar situations from their own experience.

5.   This unit emphasises once again the experience of sharing meals together. Ask the children to tell you the story of Haggle the Hungry Hag.

6.   Before you leave you might like to pray with the children.

All make the Sign of the Cross.

Priest: Let us pray together for a few moments, giving thanks
to God for having blessed us with friends.
We think of our friends at home, our parents, brothers
and sisters who love and care for us in many ways.
Let us thank God together.

All: God Our Father, we praise and thank you.

Priest: We think of our friends at school, the teacher who
helps us to learn and the other children who play with
us and share with us and make our lives in school
happy. Let us thank God together.

All: God Our Father, we praise and thank you.

Priest: For friends who play with us, for friends who help us
to explore and enjoy the countryside, for friends who
share their books, toys and sweets with us, for friends
who share food with us, let us thank God together.

All: God Our Father, we praise and thank you.

Priest: We will finish by thanking God together in the words
of the night prayer.

All: God Our Father, I come to say
thank you for your love today.
Thank you for my family
and all the friends you give to me.
Guard me in the dark of night
and in the morning send your light.
Amen.

UNIT 2
JESUS, FRIEND OF CHILDREN

The children have already been helped to get to know Jesus and
to relate to him. We now help them come to a deeper appreciation
of the great love, care, mercy and compassion that Jesus had
for all those whom he encountered. We also help them to be
more aware of the special relationship that Jesus had with the
Father. This unit also contains this year's lessons to help the
children to celebrate the birth of Jesus at Christmas.

The lessons in this unit are:

Jesus grows up in Nazareth
Jesus had many friends
The apostles were friends of Jesus
Jesus is a friend of the sick
Jesus loved God the Father
Mary is the Mother of Jesus
Jesus Christ, the Son of God, is born in Bethlehem

CLASSROOM VISITATION LINKED TO UNIT 2

1.   The first lesson in this unit once again talks about Jesus as
a child who grew, played, talked, laughed, went to school etc.
We help the children to appreciate the historical Jesus as someone
who had the capacity to experience life, to grow and to learn
as they are now doing. Ask the children to tell you about some
of the things that Jesus probably did as a child. Ask them if they
can tell you the story of the time when Jesus was lost in the
temple. How do they think Mary and Joseph felt? Did anything
like this ever happen to them? How did they feel? How did their
parents feel?

2.   Ask them if they can name some of the people who were
friends of Jesus. They may be able to talk about Peter, Matthew,
Mary, Martha, Lazarus, the apostles. They may be able to sing
a song called 'The Apostles' which lists the names of the twelve
apostles.

3.   Remind the children of the way in which Jesus related
with special love and care to those who were sick. Ask them to
tell you the story of the daughter of Jairus.

4.   Lesson 4 of this unit concentrates on Jesus' relationship
with the Father. We help the children to be aware of the
importance Jesus placed on his prayer to the Father and we
introduce them to some of the things Jesus said about the way
in which God loves and cares for all people. See pp. 79-82 of
the teacher's book. Talk to the children about these things.

5.   Before you go invite the children to pray with you the
words that Jesus taught the apostles to use when they asked him
to teach them to pray, the Our Father.

VISIT BEFORE CHRISTMAS

1.   This year the children have heard the story of Mary's visit to Elizabeth. Encourage them to tell you this story. Ask them to sing one of the songs they have learned in honour of Mary, 'Hail Mary', which is the words of the Hail Mary put to music, or 'Mary'.

2.   Tell the children the Christmas story.

3.   If the children have prepared a Christmas play or pageant they would be delighted to have you as an audience.

ADVENT
The season of Advent is an opportune time to provide the opportunity for the children to celebrate the Sacrament of Reconciliation. The teacher's book, pp.84-90, contains celebrations according to Rites I and II. The teacher would probably greatly appreciate a visit by you to the classroom to help prepare the children for the sacrament. You could revise with the children the ways in which Jesus showed love to the apostles, the children, the daughter of Jairus. Encourage them to reflect on the ways in which they have shown love to their friends:

AT HOME
sharing toys, sweets, food
helping with the housework
being alert to situations where someone is extra-tired etc.

AT SCHOOL
playing games together
helping in the classroom etc.

IN THE NEIGHBOURHOOD
picking blackberries together
going on picnics
visiting someone who is sick etc.

Encourage them to reflect on times when they have failed to show love to their friends:

AT HOME
being greedy
not helping to wash up, weed the garden
refusing to wind the baby

AT SCHOOL
not helping to tidy the classroom
not being fair at play
not allowing others to read their comics etc.

IN THE NEIGHBOURHOOD
spoiling games
quarrelling
not visiting friends who are sick etc.

Tell the children the story of Zacchaeus again.
Reflect with them on the love and forgiveness of the Father.
Encourage them to think about the way in which Zacchaeus
changed after his meeting with Jesus.
Encourage them to pray together the Act of Sorrow, and to sing
some of the hymns which they have learned on the theme of
saying sorry.

UNIT 3

JESUS SHOWS HOW FRIENDS LOVE AND FORGIVE

This unit concentrates on moral development. We help the
children come to an awareness of God's call to each one to live
in love and friendship with him and with others. We help them
to see that in his life with others Jesus showed us how we should
answer that call. Sometimes we fail to answer God's call, then
we need to be reconciled. Jesus showed us that God's forgiveness
is available to us in the Sacrament of Reconciliation. We help
the children to examine their conscience in the light of their own
experience and of the example of Jesus in the Gospel: 'Love
God'; 'Pray'; 'Love one another'; 'Forgive one another'; 'Share
with one another'; 'Speak the truth'. We encourage them to ask
themselves if they have always loved as Jesus asks them to love.
The distinction between mortal and venial sins and the necessity
of confessing moral sins in the Sacrament of Penance will be
introduced in a later class of the primary programme. In the
meantime we help the children to appreciate that certain actions
are more serious than others and that knowledge and consent
are necessary for something to be sinful.

The titles of the lessons in this unit are:

We can love
Jesus shows love

As friends of Jesus, we show love
Jesus shows the forgiveness of God Our Father
Sometimes we don't love, but we can become friends again
God Our Father forgives us in the Sacrament of Penance

CLASSROOM VISITATION LINKED TO UNIT 3

1. The children have been helped to reflect on situations which present them with a choice: they can either act in such a way that they show love and care to those around them or, on the other hand, they can be selfish and act only in their own interest. You might like to use one of the stories in Lessons 1 and 2, pp. 108-109 of the teacher's book, which are open-ended so that the children can provide their own conclusion. Encourage the children to end the story in several ways and reflect with them on the consequences of the different endings for the other people around. Alternatively, you could do the same exercise using a story of your own choice.

2. We help the children to become aware of the way in which Jesus always showed love to those around him, particularly in the way he treated the sick and the sinners.

You might like to encourage the children to tell you the story of Bartimaeus. The programme also includes a version of the story of Bartimaeus which is written in verse. You could read this with the children from their own books (pp. 32-3).

3. Ask the children to tell you stories of times when they showed love to others. You might also like to tell the children a story of a time when you showed love to somebody or when somebody else showed love to you.

4. Ask the children if they can tell you the story of Joan, the girl who sulks when her mother asks her to mind the baby, but who eventually realises that she has done wrong, says sorry and is forgiven by her mother. You could also encourage them to tell stories of times when they sulked or in some way did not show love to others.

5. Tell the children the story of Zacchaeus. This is a story with which they are now quite familiar, having heard it in the First Class/Primary 3 programme. Nevertheless, it is one which they always enjoy as they find it easy to identify with Zacchaeus. Emphasise that God is always ready to forgive them whenever they fail to love.

6. On pp. 128-131 of the teacher's book you will find a penance service which you could use with the children in preparation for the Sacrament of Penance. The teacher's book also contains celebrations of the Sacrament of Penance according to Rites I and II suitable for children at this time.

UNIT4
WE CELEBRATE THE PRESENCE OF THE LORD JESUS IN THE EUCHARIST

This unit is very similar to the unit on the Mass in First Class/Primary 3. We help the children to become more aware of the presence of the risen Jesus in their lives and to celebrate this presence in the Eucharist.

The introductory notes to Unit 5 of First Class/Primary 3 are relevant here also.

The lessons in Unit 1 are:

At Mass we come together
At Mass we listen to the words of Jesus
At Mass we remember Jesus' love for us
At Mass we give thanks
At Mass we celebrate the forgiveness of God Our Father
At Mass we share the Bread of Life
Go and live like Jesus

CLASSROOM VISITATION LINKED TO UNIT 4

One of the most helpful roles that the priest can take in relation to the unit on the Mass is to help the teacher to prepare and celebrate a class Mass with the children.

During the preparation and celebration the following are some of the points that you might stress with the children.

At Mass we are together. We celebrate together, we sing together, we pray together.

At Mass we listen to the words of Jesus. Choose one gospel story that the children are familiar with. During the celebration of the Mass allow the children to join in the homily by encouraging them to say what they heard Jesus say in the reading.

Emphasise the preparation of the gifts at the Offertory.

Remind them that during the Eucharistic Prayer we remember

the story of the Last Supper and so we are reminded of the great love that Jesus had for us and we give thanks.

Help them to reflect on the meaning of the sign of peace. Ask them, now that they have shared the sign of peace, to try to live in peace with the other children.

Help them to see that in Holy Communion the Lord Jesus comes to us and helps us to grow in friendship with him and with one another. The Lord Jesus is with them as Mass is ended helping them to go and live in peace and friendship as he called them to.

UNIT 5
JESUS CALLS US INTO FRIENDSHIP WITH GOD AND WITH OTHERS

In this unit we help the children to reflect again on the Last Supper, death and resurrection of Jesus. Jesus continued to love and care for people even when others disagreed with him and threatened him. The Father responded to the faithfulness of Jesus by raising him to new life. We help the children to understand that the death and resurrection of Jesus are not totally separate events and also that the resurrection and ascension are not merely past events but that the risen Jesus is truly present and active among us today.

The lessons in this unit are:

Some people did not want Jesus as a friend
Jesus shares a special meal with his friends
Jesus died on the cross
God Our Father raised Jesus to new life
The Lord Jesus is with us always

SCHOOL VISITATION LINKED TO UNIT 5

1.   You could bring in a palm branch. Talk about Palm Sunday. Tell the story of the triumphant entry into Jerusalem. Ask the children if the story reminds them of anything that they saw happening on TV or in the world around them. Ask them how they think Jesus felt; how they think the people felt. Talk to them about what happens in the parish liturgy on Palm Sunday.

2. Tell the children the stories of the death and resurrection of Jesus or encourage them to tell you the stories. The resurrection story in this year's programme is the story of the empty tomb. Talk to the children about the significance of the Paschal Candle which will be lit in the church on Easter Sunday morning.

3. You might like to take part with the children and the teacher in a prayer service around the cross. You will find this on p. 187 of the teacher's book, or you might like to substitute your own format for this prayer.

UNIT 6
THE HOLY SPIRIT

It is more difficult to introduce children to the Holy Spirit than it is to introduce them to the Father or the Son. The terms 'Father' and 'Son' suggest real persons. The words used to describe the Holy Spirit — breath, wind, fire, water etc. are inanimate and at this stage the children are not old enough to understand the symbolism attached to them. We try to present the Holy Spirit as a real person, like the Father and the Son; the one who helped Jesus, in his life on earth, to relate to the Father and to relate in love to all those around him; the one who helped the followers of Jesus, when he was no longer with them, to live according to the teaching of Jesus; the one who helps us today to respond to the call of Jesus in our lives.

We help the children to reflect on the experience of the action of the Holy Spirit in their own lives — experiences of peace, love, harmony, reconciliation, forgiveness, prayer.

The lessons in this unit are:

May is Mary's month
Jesus sent the Holy Spirit
The Holy Spirit shows us how to love
In baptism we become friends of the Lord Jesus
The friends of the Lord Jesus are the Church

CLASSROOM VISITATION LINKED TO UNIT 6

1. Ask the children to tell you the story of Pentecost. Encourage them to talk about the ways in which the Holy Spirit affected the lives of the apostles. The children have also heard the story of Dorcas, the dressmaker, one of the early Christians, whose

life shows the Holy Spirit at work. They will be able to tell you the story of Dorcas.

2. Encourage the children to tell about times when they feel they need the help of the Holy Spirit to enable them to do the right thing. Talk to the children about times when you feel you need the help of the Holy Spirit in your life.

3. This unit deals with Baptism as a celebration of Jesus sharing his love and friendship with us. The symbolism of the candle, the pouring of water and the baptismal shawl is explored. Talk to the children about the meaning behind the use of these in the celebration of Baptism.

Encourage the children to talk about times when they attended a Baptism ceremony.

4. Encourage the children to talk about the ways in which God shows his love for us in the beauty of summer. Ask them to talk about the things they enjoy most about summertime, about holidays. Encourage them to sing one of the songs they have learned about summer.

5. You might like to pray with the children to mark the end of the school year.

All make the Sign of the Cross.

Priest: At the end of the year we will spend a short time giving thanks to God for all his blessings.
For the many ways in which he has helped us to grow and to learn during the year:
All: God Our Father, thank you for your love.
Priest: For sending Jesus to teach us how to live and how to love:
All: God Our Father, thank you for your love.
Priest: For sending the Holy Spirit to help us to live as Jesus asks:
All: God Our Father, thank you for your love.
Priest: For the beautiful world we live in:
All: God Our Father, thank you for your love.
Priest: For friends who help us to enjoy the world:
All: God Our Father, thank you for your love.

(Encourage the children to pray spontaneously, mentioning some of the things that they want particularly to thank God for.)

Final Prayer: Our Father ...

THIRD CLASS/PRIMARY 5

Teacher's Book: *Walk in Love*

Pupil's Book: *Remember me together*

Background to the approach in the Third Class/Primary 5 programme

Eight-year-olds are just beginning to emerge from the ego-centric world of the small child. They are becoming more aware of other people and are beginning to be aware of their existence as part of different groups: at home, at school, in the neighbourhood. We try to broaden this awareness to give a sense of belonging which would include all people. We use their experience of being part of groups to help them to begin to understand the community of the Church. We help them to reflect on the moral implications of living with others and to apply these to their own experience at home, in school and in the neighbourhood. We also help them to reflect on the ways in which we celebrate in the community of the Church. In this programme we look at the Sacraments of Reconciliation, Eucharist and Baptism.

There are six units in this year's programme:

Living in community
The Christian community
Living in the Christian community
We celebrate
The Holy Spirit is with the Christian community

UNIT 1
LIVING IN COMMUNITY

In this unit we explore the neighbourhood where the children live and the children's sense of belonging in their local community. We help them come to a deeper awareness of their need for other people and we encourage them to reflect on the ways in which their lives are enriched by others. Living with others involves sharing, co-operation, being prepared to think first of the needs of others, being open to acknowledge and value the gifts and talents of others. We help them to reflect on the implications of these for their lives with others. We also help them become aware of people in other parts of the world whose experience of life and whose customs and ways of life are very different from ours. We help them to respect these differences. We also try to bring them to an awareness of the interdependence of all people and so to a sense of responsibility even for those who live in distant parts of the world.

The lessons in this unit are:

Our neighbourhood
Our community
Needing others
Working together
Getting to know other people

CLASSROOM VISITATION LINKED TO UNIT 1

1. In the first lesson of this unit, we help the children to focus on the neighbourhood where they live, so that they will appreciate all that it offers to them and will therefore want to respect and improve it. You could talk to the children about the places in the neighbourhood which appeal in a particular way to you. Encourage them to tell you about some place that they particularly like to visit. What do they do when they go there? Why do they like it? etc.

2. Encourage the children to talk about living with other people at home, at school, in the neighbourhood — Who are these people? What do they enjoy doing together? How do they help one another?
From the programme they might like to tell you the story about 'Happy times in Ballymacnab' or 'The sports day'. Encourage the children to talk about times when they felt lonely, sad or frightened. Talk to them about the need we have for other people at times such as these. From the programme they may be able to tell you the story of 'The four wishes' or 'Bread and milk for Ballyskelligs'.

4. We encourage the children to appreciate the values of sharing and co-operation and to see that in their lives with others they need to put these into practice. There is a story entitled 'The stone and the stranger' on p. 61 of the teacher's book. This story explores the difference between sharing and hoarding and between working in co-operation with others and in isolation. You could read this story to the children. The following questions will help them to talk about it.

How do you think the people felt when there was no food in the town?

Why did the people in the story decide to keep whatever food they had for themselves?

Did you ever see people acting in this way?

Did you ever do anything like what the people in the story did?

How did things change when the stranger came?

What caused the change to happen?

Did you ever see people acting as those in the story did after the stranger had spoken to them?

Did you ever act in this way?

What would change in our world if people acted like this more often?

5. We introduced the children to the fact that people who live in other countries practise different customs from us, have different lifestyles, speak different languages, wear different clothes. We help them to appreciate that we are inter-dependent and also responsible for one another's welfare. If you have visited a Third World country talk to the children about that experience. Encourage the children to talk about people they know who are working in these countries. If there are people from their parish working on the missions mention their names.

Encourage the children to talk about some of the foods that we buy from these countries and about some of the items which we send to other countries.

6. Encourage the children to sing some of the songs they learned in this unit.

7. The following may help you to pray with the children before you leave.

All make the Sign of the Cross.

Priest: There are many things for which we can give thanks to God.

	Let us spend some time thinking of these, thanking God for them, and asking him to help us to use them as we should.
	We live in a neighbourhood where there are many beautiful and useful things. We'll mention some of them and give thanks to God together. (Encourage the children to mention some of the beautiful and useful things in their neighbourhood.)
Priest:	Let us give thanks to the Lord Our God.
All:	It is right to give him thanks and praise.
Priest:	We remember all the people in our lives who help us: those we live with at home, those in school, those we meet in the neighbourhood. Let us think of the many ways in which they help us to be happy. We will mention some of them and thank God for them. (Encourage the children to mention some of these people by name.)
Priest:	Let us give thanks to the Lord Our God.
All:	It is right to give him thanks and praise.
Priest:	We think of those who live in far-off countries who often don't have enough to eat or drink. We think of the people who are working with them. We thank God for them.
Priest:	Let us give thanks to the Lord Our God.
All:	It is right to give him thanks and praise.
Priest:	God Our Father, help us to treat the place where we live with respect and care. Help us to share and co-operate with the people with whom we live.
	Let us pray together in the words Jesus taught us.
All:	Our Father...

UNIT 2
JESUS AND HIS COMMUNITY

In this unit we help the children to come to know more about the way in which Jesus grew up and lived in his neighbourhood and community. He helped people to live in peace and love for God and for one another. He showed people, in his own life and in the stories he told, how to share, how to care for one another and how to forgive.

The lessons in this unit are:

Jesus lived in Nazareth
Jesus loved the Father
Jesus loved people
The apostles followed Jesus

CLASSROOM VISITATION LINKED TO UNIT 2

1.   We help the children to relate to Jesus as someone who grew
and learned as they are doing. We help them to reflect on some
of the things that probably influenced Jesus as a child which later
became significant in his preaching and teaching. Encourage the
children to talk about the things Jesus noticed in the countryside
as he grew up: the farmers, the shepherds, the market place.
Ask them if they can remember any of the prayers which Jesus
probably learned as a child.

2.   Ask the children to talk about some of the things which
Jesus told the people about the Father. Tell them the story of
Jesus meeting the buyers and sellers in the temple. Encourage
them to talk about the reasons why Jesus was angry.

3.   In this unit we revise some of the stories the children have
already heard which show the love and care Jesus had for people,
especially those who were sick or despised. You could ask them
to tell you the story of Bartimaeus, or of the daughter of Jairus.
We introduce them to Amos the leper in story, song and verse.
You could encourage them to tell you this story. Encourage them
to talk about how Amos felt before and after he met Jesus. Ask
them to think about times when they, or others whom they know
felt like this.

4.   Ask the children to talk about their experience of leaders
in the games they play. Encourage them to talk about the qualities
that make a good leader. You could also encourage them to talk
about people who are leaders in the world. Ask them to tell you
the stories of 'The storm at sea' and 'The argument about the
greatest'. Encourage them to reflect on the way in which Jesus
acted as a leader in these stories. Tell them the story of 'The call
of Matthew'. Reflect with them on the question of whether it
was easy to have Jesus as a leader.

5.   Starting on p.103 of the teacher's book there is a reflective
prayer service based on the story of Jesus and the leper Amos.
You might like to use this with the children or, alternatively,

you might like to use any of the other stories the children have heard in this unit as the basis for a reflective prayer. This type of reflective prayer based on the stories of Jesus can help to deepen the children's relationship with Jesus. It can also help them to become more familiar with silent prayer.

UNIT 3
THE CHRISTIAN COMMUNITY

In this unit we help the children to begin to see themselves as members of the community of the Church. We help them to understand that the risen Jesus is with us in the Church, as we try to live together as a community of his followers. As our starting point we take the children's experience of life in the Church. In this unit too we deepen the children's understanding of the Sacraments of Baptism and Eucharist.

The lessons in this unit are:

We follow Jesus
We are welcomed into the Christian community — Baptism
Christmas — Jesus comes for all people
At Mass we celebrate
As Mass we are united in love

CLASSROOM VISITATION LINKED TO UNIT 3

1. The children have heard the story of Mother Teresa as someone who tries to live as a follower of Jesus, by doing the same kind of things as he did to help people, especially those who are suffering, to live a more human life. Encourage them to talk about Mother Teresa. You could tell them about people you know who try to live as followers of Jesus.

In a lead-up to the lesson on the Sacrament of Baptism we help the children to think about what it means to begin to belong to a new group. Encourage them to talk about groups that they belong to: how they joined, what they have to do to continue to belong. Talk through the Rite of Baptism with them, helping them to understand the significance of the different symbols used and the various parts of the ritual.

3. The teaching on the Mass in this unit centres on the Mass as commemoration of the death and resurrection of Jesus and

celebration of his presence and action among us today. We help them, too, to appreciate that the Bread of Life, which we receive at Mass, strengthens our relationship with the risen Jesus and with one another.

The children benefit greatly from the experience of celebrating a class Mass. If possible, the best time for such a celebration in Third Class/Primary 5 is in the context of this unit. A possible outline of a class Mass is included in the teacher's book starting on p.180. Your involvement with the teacher and children in the preparation of the Mass would help greatly.

The first lesson on the Mass in this unit goes through the different parts of the Mass with the children and helps them to understand the meaning behind what we do and say.

This could be reinforced for the children during their experience of taking part in the Mass in a manner suited to their age, experience and level of understanding, e.g. you could introduce each part of the Mass with a few short words, for example: In the Confiteor we pray together at the beginning of Mass. We confess that we have done wrong. We ask God and our neighbour to forgive us.

It is important to involve the children in a participative way, in so far as is possible, both in the preparation and celebration — they can help choose the readings, they can make their own prayers of the faithful etc.

4.   The programme also contains on p. 147 of the teacher's book a celebration of the Sacrament of Penance suitable for this class during the season of Advent. There is also a penance service.

UNIT 4
LIVING IN THE CHRISTIAN COMMUNITY

In this unit we focus mainly on moral development. We introduce the children to Jesus' law of love. We help them to relate this to the everyday situations which occur in their own lives. Jesus showed us in his life what it means to live according to his law of love. We use the term 'living in the new way' to describe this. We also help the children to come to an awareness of the ways in which they fail to live up to this teaching of Jesus — then they live in 'the old way'. We help them to see themselves as people who sin, to become more aware of the call to repent and to experience at a deeper level the process through which we are reconciled with God and with one another. In most dioceses this is the first occasion when the Sacrament of Penance is celebrated according to Rite I — this is included on p. 54 of the pupil's book.

The lessons in this unit are:

Jesus asks us to live in the New Way
Jesus asks us to love others
The saints lived as Jesus asked them to
Lent — Jesus asks us to leave the Old Way behind
The risen Jesus shows us the forgiveness of the Father in the Sacrament of Penance

CLASSROOM VISITATION LINKED TO UNIT 4

1.   The first lesson presents many stories of situations which show what happens when people live in the 'new way' and when people live in the 'old way'. Many of these stories are open-ended and so encourage discussion among the children about different options and the consequences of these options. All of these stories present situations which are relevant in terms of the ordinary everyday experiences of children of this age group.

You will find these stories on pp. 191-6 of the teacher's book, or you may like to use stories which you can make up yourself. This can be a useful starting point from which the children can proceed to talk about times when they live in the 'new way' and times when they live in the 'old way'.

The children hear for the first time the story of the Good Samaritan in which Jesus spoke about someone who lived in the 'new way'. You might like to tell the children this story or you could encourage them to tell you the story. You could encourage them to read together from their own books a poem which paints a picture of a modern parallel to the story of the Good Samaritan.

2.   We help the children to reflect on the implications of Jesus' call to live in the 'new way' in relation to three specific areas of their lives: respect for others; honesty and truthfulness; peace. You could use the stories on pp. 43-45 of their own book to start a discussion on these. Encourage the children to talk about their own experience of trying to live according to these values, the difficulty involved and times when they failed.

3. Saint Francis of Assisi, Saint Patrick and Saint Margaret of Scotland are presented as examples of people who lived as Jesus asked them to.

You could encourage the children to tell you these stories. Alternatively, you might like to tell them a story of someone you know whose life was an example of living in love for God and for others.

4. We assure the children that even when they sin, God always loves them and that he is always ready to welcome them back into his friendship. The programme here presents the story of the prodigal son. You could tell them this story, or you might like to encourage them to tell you the story, or to dramatise the story for you. You might also like to encourage them to read the poem about the Loving Father on pp. 48-49 of their own books.

We help the children to be aware of the many ways in which we can return to God when we have sinned:
— the Penitential Rite at Mass
— by praying the Act of Sorrow
— by telling God in our own words that we are sorry for having sinned
— during Lent, when we are reminded with the rest of the community to do penance
— by celebrating the Sacrament of Reconciliation

It is good to remind the children of these and to assure them that God is always ready to forgive them.

In this programme emphasis is placed on the celebration of the Sacrament of Reconciliation according to Rite I. We help the children to reflect on the process of reconciliation in their own experience: acknowledgement of guilt, saying sorry, being forgiven, being reconciled.

Encourage them to tell stories of times when they said sorry and of times when they forgave somebody else for the wrong that was done to them. The programme introduces the story of the denial of Peter. You might like to tell this story, emphasising that even those who were closest of all to Jesus sometimes failed and that Jesus was ready to forgive them. It is important to provide opportunities for the children to celebrate the Sacrament of Reconciliation in an atmosphere where they can really experience the love and mercy of God.

UNIT 5
WE CELEBRATE

In this unit we explore the children's experience of the Christian community's celebrations at Easter. We also help them to understand the Christian community's celebration of the presence of the risen Jesus in the sacraments, with special emphasis on the Sacrament of the Sick. We also help the children to come to an appreciation of the special role of Mary, the mother of Jesus in the Christian community. We introduce them to the five joyful mysteries of the Rosary.

The lessons in this unit are:

We celebrate the Last Supper
We remember Jesus' love for us
We celebrate the Resurrection of Jesus
We celebrate the presence of the risen Jesus in the sacraments
The Sacrament of the Sick
Mary our Mother

CLASSROOM VISITATION LINKED TO UNIT 5

1.   You could encourage the children to talk about the different times when they celebrate in their families. Ask them to describe what they do when they celebrate in their families.

2.   During a pre-Easter visit to the classroom it is always a good idea to tell again the stories of the Last Supper, Passion, Death and Resurrection of Jesus. This year the programme includes the story of the washing of the feet and the resurrection story used is the story of the meeting on the road to Emmaus. The children will join you in the telling of these stories.

They have also learned a number of hymns appropriate to this time of year: 'Jesus took Bread'; 'Stay with me'; 'He is Lord'. They may be able to sing some of these.

3.   Talk to the children about the significance of the Paschal Candle which they will notice in the church on Easter Sunday morning.

4.   Ask the children if they can name the seven sacraments. Encourage them to talk about the special events in the lives of people which are celebrated in the different sacraments.

5. Encourage the children to talk about being sick and about those who care for them when they are sick. Encourage them to tell you the story of Tom Dooley which they have learned in the programme. Talk to them about the way in which Jesus cared for those who were sick. You might like to ask them to tell you some stories about people to whom Jesus showed love and care when they were sick. Talk to the children about the Sacrament of the Sick as a way in which the Church shows care today for those who are sick.

6. You could ask the children to name the five joyful mysteries of the Rosary. Encourage them to tell the stories connected with these.

7. If you would like to pray with the children it might be appropriate to say a mystery of the Rosary with them. They could finish by singing one of the songs they have learned in honour of Mary.

UNIT 6
THE HOLY SPIRIT IS WITH THE CHRISTIAN COMMUNITY

In this unit we help the children to come to a better understanding of the Holy Spirit. We talk about the Holy Spirit as someone who is present in the life of Jesus, in the early Christian community and in the lives of people in the Church today.

The lessons in this unit are:

The Lord Jesus sends his Spirit
The Holy Spirit helps Christians
In summer we enjoy God's world

CLASSROOM VISITATION LINKED WITH UNIT 6

1. We start by helping the children to become aware of their experience of the action of the Holy Spirit in the lives of people around them. The programme tells a story about a community who collected money to send a sick boy to Lourdes. You could encourage the children to talk about ways in which they have noticed the Holy Spirit helping people in their community to care for one another. Tell them the story of Pentecost. Reflect

with them on the effect the Holy Spirit had on the lives of the apostles. This unit gives many stories of people in whose lives we see the Holy Spirit at work — Peter, Catherine McAuley, Edel Quinn, today's missionaries.

You could tell a story of someone you know or knew about whose life shows the work of the Holy Spirit.

3. Since this will be the last visit of the year you might like to end with a prayer.

All make the Sign of the Cross.

Priest: Let us thank God together for all his blessings during the past year.
For all we have learned, Father we thank you.
All: Blessed be God.
Priest: For the different communities we live with, at home, at school, in the neighbourhood; for people who love and care for us, who encourage us, who are our friends, Father we thank you.
All: Blessed be God.
Priest: For the gift of summertime, for long days and for holidays, for sunshine and for fun, Father we thank you.
All: Blessed be God.
Priest: For the gift of the Holy Spirit who helps us to live as Jesus asked us, Father we thank you.
All: Blessed be God.

(The prayer could conclude with one of the songs the children have learned, e.g. 'Beautiful Things'.)

FOURTH CLASS/PRIMARY 6

Teacher's Book: *Grow in Love*

Pupil's Book: *A Time to Grow*

Background to the approach in the Fourth Class/Primary 6 programme

We have chosen the experience of growth for this year's programme. Children at this level, round about age nine, are capable of reflecting on the growth that is taking place in their own bodies and in the world around them. They are growing physically, emotionally, morally. They are still incapable of understanding abstract ideas but are beginning to have the capacity to appreciate the world of symbol.

There are five units in this year's programme:

God Our Father is calling us to grow
Jesus helped people to grow
We can grow in love
At Mass the risen Jesus helps us to grow
We grow together in the Spirit of the risen Jesus

UNIT 1
GOD OUR FATHER IS CALLING US TO GROW

In this unit we help the children to reflect upon and to become more aware of the growth that is taking place in their bodies, in their minds and in their relationships with others. We help them to realise that this capacity for growth is a gift from God and that God calls each individual to grow. We encourage them to become aware of the skills and talents they possess and to use these for their own growth, the growth of others and the development of the world around them. In helping the children to have confidence in themselves, to appreciate their own worth and dignity and to relate to others we lay down foundations for their ongoing moral development. We help them to see themselves in partnership with God in the ongoing work of creation in their own bodies and in the world around them.

The lessons in this unit are:

Growing
We are loved. We grow
Growing is exciting
Our love helps others to grow

CLASSROOM VISITATION LINKED TO UNIT 1

1. On your first visit of the year you could welcome the children back after the summer holidays. This year it is particularly appropriate to remark on the way in which they have grown since you last saw them. Encourage them to tell you about their summer holidays. You might like to tell them about an incident from your summer holidays.

2. Ask the children to sing the song 'Growing Up' from Lesson 1 of this unit. Encourage them to talk about the things that help them to grow. To start this discussion you could refer to any of the stories in Lesson 2 of the teacher's book — Queen Annabel, John's Cake, A Friendship, Gillian's Bicycle.

3. On p. 7 of the pupil's book there is a prayer which gives thanks to God for people who, in different ways, help us to grow; you might like to pray this with the children.

4. Encourage the children to talk about the most exciting thing that has happened to them because of the way in which they have grown — it may be that they are able to do something now that they enjoy very much, e.g. go fishing, play the piano etc. You might tell them about the things which you learned that gave you most pleasure and satisfaction.

5. In this unit we encourage the children to become aware of their duty to help others to grow — especially those who live in Third World countries. The children will probably enjoy singing the song 'Harambee'.

You could read for the children the story of Kamba on p. 61 of the teacher's book or of Assita on p. 64. Encourage them to talk about the things needed by people in Third World countries and which we take for granted. Ask them to talk about ways in which they can help people in Third World countries.

7. You could use the prayer on p. 11 of the pupil's book as a starting point for a prayer service to end your visit.

UNIT 2
JESUS HELPED PEOPLE TO GROW

In this unit we help the children to see how Jesus helps us to grow in love of God and of others. He helps us to grow by his life when he shows us how to live and how to love. He helps us to grow by the stories he told. Through prayer we help the children to relate to Jesus Christ as someone who is present and active in their lives, calling them and enabling them to grow.

The lessons in this unit are:

Jesus grows up
Jesus and the apostles
Jesus and the woman at the well
Jesus told stories which helped people to grow
People learned through being with Jesus
Jesus shows us how to love God the Father

CLASSROOM VISITATION LINKED TO UNIT 2

1. We help the children to come to know more about the way in which Jesus, as a child, grew in relationship with God and with others. Encourage the children to tell you some of the Bible stories that Jesus learned as a boy. They may also be able to tell you some of the prayers he learned, how he celebrated the Sabbath, how he celebrated the feast of the Passover. They may also be able to talk about his pilgrimage visit to Jerusalem at the age of twelve.

2. We help the children to appreciate how Jesus, through his presence with them and his love for them, helped the apostles to change and to grow. We repeat some of the stories which the children have already heard in programmes from previous years. Jesus' love for the world of nature, the argument about who was the greatest, the call of Matthew. You could encourage them to tell and to talk about any of the stories or, alternatively, you could tell them the story and then encourage them to talk about it, e.g. the story of Matthew on p. 115 of the pupil's book.

3. In the story of the woman at the well we focus on the way in which the love and acceptance of Jesus transformed the people's lives. As well as learning the story, the children have learned a song and a poem about the woman at the well. You could use any of these to help the children to discuss the story. Encourage them to talk about how the woman felt before and after she met Jesus; to imagine themselves in the woman's shoes; to recall other Bible stories they have heard with a similar theme, e.g. Zacchaeus. You might like to pray with the children using the prayerful reflection on p.19 of the pupil's book.

4. We present the following stories which Jesus told, all with the theme of 'growing': The mustard seed; The unforgiving servant; The two sons; The dough and the yeast. We encourage the children to reflect on these stories and on the way in which the stories relate to their own lives. You could either tell some of the stories to the children or encourage them to tell you the stories.

5. We help the children to reflect on the way in which Jesus treated people and on some of the things he said, through the following stories: The ten lepers; Jesus defends his Father's house; Zacchaeus; The widow.
You could tell the story of the ten lepers and encourage them to think what it was that those who were with Jesus learned from the way in which he treated the lepers and from things he said to the one who returned. They could read for you the poem entitled 'The Widow's Treasure' on p.25 of their own book. Encourage them to talk about how the apostles were influenced by the way in which Jesus reacted to the widow's offering.

6. We help the children to reflect on the way in which Jesus helped people to relate to the Father. Encourage them to tell you some of the things they have learned which Jesus said about God. You could talk to them about the deep relationship that Jesus himself had with the Father, his awareness of being close to the Father, his prayer to the Father.

7. We help the children to reflect on the meaning behind the first three phrases of the Our Father. As a closing prayer you could pray these slowly with the children and reflect with them on the significance of the words, e.g.

Our Father, who art in heaven;
God is our Father.
He loves us very much.

Hallowed be thy name;
Blessed be the name of God.
Holy is the name of God.
Praised be the name of God.
Glory be to the name of God.
Great is the name of God.
Wonderful is the name of God.

Thy will be done;
May whatever God wants be done.
May we do what God wants.
May we pray to him and praise him.
May we love one another as he wants us to.

UNIT 3
WE CAN GROW IN LOVE

In this unit we concentrate on moral development. We help the
children to increase their awareness of God's call to grow in love.
We help them to reflect on their capacity to choose to respond
to God's call in their own lives. We help them to become aware
that we are responsible for the consequences of our own choices.
God calls us to make good choices. Jesus shows us how to make
good choices. It is difficult to choose as Jesus asks. When we
deliberately choose not to follow the example of Jesus, which,
in this unit, is summed up in his commandment of love: 'Love
the Lord your God with all your heart and with all your mind
and your neighbour as yourself', we sin. We help the children
to see that we are all sinners and need God's mercy and
forgiveness. We stress God's love for humankind: God so loved
the world that he sent his Son to save it. The underlying theme
of this unit is salvation. God continually calls us to repentance
and conversion. God's mercy and compassion always await us.
God's forgiveness is absolute and unconditional. This unit
prepares the children for a celebration of the Sacrament of
Penance.

The lessons in this unit are:

We can choose
The Lord Jesus calls us to make good choices
We make selfish choices. We refuse to grow
It is difficult to make good choices
Saved from selfishness
Jesus saved people from selfishness
Jesus is the light of the world

CLASSROOM VISITATION LINKED TO UNIT 3

1.   You could begin a discussion on our capacity to make choices by using one of the incidents on p.28 of the pupil's book. Encourage the children to talk about the options that are possible, to reflect on which one is the easiest, to decide which is the right choice, to think about times in their experience when they had the opportunity to make choices. You could tell them about a situation when you were faced with the possibility of making a choice, talk about the way in which you made your decision, what influenced it etc. You could ask them to read the poem 'Choice' from p. 29 of their own book. Reflect with them on the advantages of being able to choose.

2.   We present the story of the Good Samaritan as one Jesus told which gave the people an opportunity to reflect on making choices and on the consequences of the choices we make. You could tell them the story or encourage them to tell you the story. Reflect with them on the reasons why the different characters in the story chose as they did.

We sum up the call of Jesus to make good choices in the law of love: 'Love the Lord your God with all your heart, with all your soul, with all your strength and with all your mind and your neighbour as yourself.' We also give the children a set of guidelines for making good choices: love God; respect God's name; pray; respect myself; respect others; be truthful; be honest; share with others; wish everybody well. You could talk to the children about these. Encourage them to tell you what each means in relation to the way in which they live their lives. You might like to read slowly and prayerfully with the children the reflection on p.30 of the pupil's book.

3. On p. 33 of the pupil's book there are captions which refer to incidents that happened because people made bad choices. You could look at these with the children and encourage them to talk about the reasons why people made bad choices and about the results of their actions.

You might like to read and discuss the stories on p. 34 of the pupil's book, stories of incidents that happened when people made selfish choices. Encourage the children to talk to you about times when they made selfish choices. You could talk to them about times when you made selfish choices. Talk to the children about the fact that we all, at times, make bad choices, that because of this there is evil in the world, that God sent his Son Jesus Christ to show us how to overcome evil and to assure us that God will always forgive us when we fail.

4. You could tell the children the story of 'The twins' birthday' from p. 146 of the teacher's book, which deals with the difficulty of making good choices. Alternatively, you might like to tell them a story, from your own experience, of a time when you found it very difficult to make the right choice. Encourage them to tell you similar stories from their own experience.

5. We introduce the children to the fact that Jesus came to save people from sin and selfishness. In order to help them to understand the concept of Saviour we tell them two stories — 'Father Flanagan of Boystown' and 'Mr Brigin' which you will find on pp.151 and 152 of the teacher's book. You could encourage them to tell these stories: and to talk about the way in which, in each of the stories, people were saved from the situations they were in. Read with the children the story of the woman who was a sinner from pp. 36 and 37 of the pupil's book. Encourage them to talk about the way in which Jesus helped the woman to change. You might like to ask them to sing the hymn 'My Shepherd is the Lord'.

6. To help the children to reflect again on the mercy and forgiveness of God, which Jesus showed us, we tell the story of the prodigal son and the story of the unforgiving servant.

Impress upon them the all-embracing nature of the love and mercy of God. This could be part of a preparation for the Sacrament of Penance. You could help the children to examine their conscience in the light of the rules they have learned for making good choices, e.g. Jesus calls us to be honest. Let us think about our lives with others at home, at school, in the neighbourhood. Have there been times when we took things which didn't belong to us? Jesus calls us to be truthful. Have there been times when we told lies to our parents at home, to our teachers or the other children in school, to our friends in the neighbourhood? etc.

CHRISTMAS VISIT

1. This year we introduce children to the notion of Jesus as the light of the world. Encourage the children to talk about the properties of light. Talk to them about the reasons why we call Jesus the light of the world. Talk to them about the Irish custom of placing a lighted candle in the window at Christmas.

2. If the children have practised a play or pageant based on the Christmas story ask them to act it out for you. Alternatively, they could tell you the story of the birth of Jesus at Christmas.

3. Encourage them to sing some of the Christmas hymns they know.

4. Invite them to visit the crib in the parish church during the Christmas season.

UNIT 4
AT MASS THE RISEN JESUS HELPS US TO GROW

In this unit we help the children to come to a deeper awareness of the presence of the risen Jesus with them in their lives and especially in the Mass. We help them to see that when they go to Mass, listen to God's word, remember and confess their sinfulness, receive the Bread of Life in Holy Communion etc., the risen Jesus helps us to go from Mass to live and love as he asks us to.

In this unit too we help the children once more to reflect on the Passion, Death and Resurrection of Jesus.

The lessons in this unit are:

At Mass we grow when we listen
At Mass we grow through giving and receiving
At Mass we grow when we say sorry and make peace
At Mass the risen Jesus helps us to grow

The Last Supper
Jesus died for us
God the Father raised Jesus to new life
Jesus is Lord
The Lord Jesus is with us always
Mary grew through listening to God

CLASSROOM VISITATION LINKED WITH THE MASS

It is always most helpful when the priest helps the children and the teacher to prepare for and celebrate Mass in the classroom.

On p. 246 of the teacher's book there is an indication of a possible text for the Mass which would tie in with the theme of growth in this year's programme. You could, however, with the teacher and the children choose other material which would also be suitable.

You could talk to the children about the various parts of the Mass. Encourage them to tell you what they have already learned, e.g.

THE PENITENTIAL RITE
In the Penitential Rite we remember our sinfulness. We think of the bad choices we made. We say sorry. We are helped to grow when we realise and acknowledge that we have done wrong.

THE READINGS
In the readings we listen to the word of God.

The programme suggests the story of David and the prophet Nathan as a First Reading and the story of the mustard seed for the Gospel. Help the children to think about the way in which we can grow when we listen to these stories.

THE OFFERTORY
We explore with the children the concept of giving at a deeper level. We help them to see that sometimes we can give others non-material gifts: the gift of love, the gift of oneself. The best gifts are not necessarily those which are most costly. On pp. 196 and 197 of the teacher's book there is a story entitled 'The best gift' and a poem, 'The present', both of which emphasise that love is the best gift of all.

Talk to the children about our celebration of Mass as a time when we remember that Jesus gave himself fully to those around him and that he gave himself fully to the Father. At Mass the risen Jesus continues to give himself to us and to the Father and we give ourselves to God with him.

THE SIGN OF PEACE
At the Sign of Peace we remember that Jesus asked his followers to live in peace with one another. We shake hands with the people near us to show that we want to live in peace as Jesus asks. Having done this we must try to live it out in our lives when Mass is over.

WE RECEIVE THE BREAD OF LIFE IN HOLY COMMUNION
You could read for the children the story of the loaves and fishes as it appears on pp. 212 and 213 of the teacher's book. When we receive the Bread of Life in Holy Communion it helps us to grow closer to Jesus and to God. Show the children some altar breads. Explain that this is real bread. When the priest blesses it at the consecration and remembers what Jesus did at the Last Supper it becomes the Bread of Life which is the Lord Jesus.

During a celebration of Mass in the classroom it is possible to relate what the children are actually doing to what they have already learned about the Mass. Encourage as high a level of participation among the children as possible.

EASTER VISIT
1. Encourage the children to tell you the stories of the Last Supper, death and resurrection of Jesus. The resurrection story in this year's programme is the story of the meeting between Thomas and the risen Jesus (John 20, Luke 24).

2. Talk to the children about the ceremony of the veneration of the cross in the Good Friday liturgy.

3. Talk to the children about the significance of the Paschal Candle in the church on Easter Sunday.

4. Reflect with the children on the continuing presence of the risen Jesus with us in our lives. You might like to use the prayerful reflection on p. 61 of the pupil's book.

VISIT DURING THE MONTH OF MAY
1. In the Fourth Class/Primary 6 programme we help the children to come to know Mary as a woman of great strength and courage. We link feast days in honour of Mary to the stories of the events from her life which the feast day commemorates. You could talk about 8 September, 8 December, 1 January and 15 August as special days when we honour Mary.

2. We introduce the children to the story of Lourdes as a place where people, in a special way, pay tribute to Mary. You could tell the children about trips which you have made to Lourdes. If any of the children have been to Lourdes they could tell the story of the visit.

3. Before you leave you could gather the children around the May altar to pray together a mystery of the Rosary.

UNIT 5
WE GROW TOGETHER IN THE SPIRIT OF THE RISEN JESUS

In this unit we help the children to deepen their awareness of the presence of the risen Jesus in their lives, through his Spirit. We present the Holy Spirit as the advocate, who was sent to the apostles at Pentecost and who transformed their whole lives, as the one who is sent to us at Baptism and who helps us to grow, as the one who, down through the ages, has helped people in the Church to live their lives as followers of the risen Jesus.

The lessons in this unit are:

The apostles grew in the Spirit of the risen Jesus
The Holy Spirit helps us to grow as children of God
In Baptism we are called to grow
We grow together in the community of the Church

CLASSROOM VISITATION LINKED WITH UNIT 5

1. The children have heard the story of the coming of the Holy Spirit on the apostles at Pentecost and also the story of the conversion of St Paul. You could ask the children to tell you these stories or you could tell them the stories. Encourage the children to talk about the effect the Holy Spirit had on the lives of the people in these stories.

2. We help the children to realise that we can know when the Holy Spirit is at work in people's lives because we can recognise the fruits of the Spirit. You could ask the children to open their books at p. 66, and to read together the passage on the fruits of the Holy Spirit. Encourage them to tell you the story of Damien of Molokai.

You could tell them a story about someone you know whose actions and lifestyle show the fruits of the Spirit, perhaps, e.g. your own parents. Encourage them to tell you of incidents where they saw the fruits of the Spirit in someone's life, e.g. when someone was particularly kind, when someone tried to make peace, when someone showed love for another etc. You could use the prayer service on p. 78 of the pupil's book to pray with the children. Ask the children to sing one of the hymns they have learned to the Holy Spirit.

3. You could talk to the children about the symbolism of water and light in Baptism. Help them to see Baptism as a time when we are called to grow and when we receive the Holy Spirit who helps us to grow. If any of them have attended a Baptism ceremony recently, encourage them to talk about what happened.

4. Encourage the children to tell you stories of the lives of people who, with the help of the Holy Spirit, grew as members of the community of the Church. They have heard the stories of Augustine, Teresa of Avila and John XXIII.

FIFTH CLASS/PRIMARY 7

Teacher's Book: *Workers for the Kingdom*

Pupil's Book: *Your Kingdom Come*

Background to the approach in the Fifth Class/Primary 7 programme

The theme of this year's programme is building and making. Children of ten are beginning to discover their own talents for making and building. We use this experience as the starting point to explore the ongoing creative presence of God in the world, in nature and especially in people whom he calls to be co-creators with him.

UNIT 1
CREATION

In this unit we help the children to become more aware of their own gifts and talents and of the gifts and talents of those around them. We help them to understand that God calls them to use these gifts and talents in co-operation with others, to make the world a better place for all. We help them to realise that they are responsible for the development of their own gifts and talents. We help them to appreciate the work, skills and talents of other people. From the beginning people have sometimes used their gifts and talents destructively rather than creatively. We explore with them the consequences of such actions and help them to see that when we use our own gifts and talents destructively evil comes into the world through us. We introduce them to the story of creation from the Book of Genesis and to the story of the Fall, trying to ensure that they have some understanding of the literary form used in these writings.

We help them come to a deep appreciation of God's work of creation and to be aware of his call to us to treat all creation with respect and reverence.

The lessons in this unit are:

We build. We create
We live. We create
The living world
Creation comes from God
Working for a better world
Refusing to follow God's way

CLASSROOM VISITATION LINKED WITH UNIT 1

1. The unit begins by helping the children to come to an awareness of their own gifts and talents. Through reflecting on their experience, we help them to see that it is often through other people's help and encouragement that it is possible for us to become aware of and to develop our own gifts and talents. You could ask them to talk about the 'Scottish legend' which is included on p. 2 of the pupil's book. You could talk to them about things you have noticed which indicate some of their gifts and talents, e.g. the art work on the walls, the games they play, their singing in the church etc.

2. Encourage the children to talk about the various signs that they can see in the world around which show that the work of creation in the world is ongoing, e.g. the birth of a baby; new life in the world of nature etc.

Talk to them about the fact that it is easiest for us to grow and develop our talents when we do so with the co-operation of others. There are many stories which illustrate this. In their programme there is the story of Nigel Hunt. But the children may also have heard about Christy Brown and Christopher Nolan. Alternatively, you could tell them about someone you know who grew and developed because of the help received from others. The children may also like to talk about people who developed their skills and talents to an extraordinarily high degree and used them for the benefit of others, e.g. Alexander Graham Bell, Michelangelo etc. Talk to them about the fact that we all have gifts and talents, that we are all called to develop these to the fullest potential possible and to use them for our own benefit and to make the world a better place for all people.

3. Talk to the children about the beauty of the world and about the ways in which you are reminded of the beauty, power and creativity of God when you look at the beauty of the earth.

Encourage them to talk to you about the ways in which they enjoy the beauty of the earth. You might like to read together the translation of Psalm 65 which you will find on p. 9 of the pupil's book.

4. You could ask the children to tell you the 'Legend of the Rainbow' or they could read it for you from p. 40 of the pupil's book.

Encourage them to discuss what the story says about co-operation, about working in isolation, about recognising the importance of gifts and talents other than our own. You could ask them if they have ever seen something happen similar to that which happened in the story, or if they have ever felt like acting as the colours did in the story. You could read for them the story of creation from the Book of Genesis. Encourage them to tell you the main things which this story tries to convey about God, about the world, about people. You could pray with them by using the prayerful reflection on p. 12 of the pupil's book. Encourage them to sing the hymn 'All the ends of the earth'.

5. Encourage the children to talk about ways in which they can use their talents to make the world a better place: in their homes; in their neighbourhoods; for people in Third World countries. You could tell them the story of an incident which you observed or took part in, where an action on the part of some one person or a group of people improved conditions for others. Encourage the children to sing the song 'Children of the universe'.

6. Encourage the children to talk about ways in which people sometimes use their talents destructively and bring evil into the world. You could talk about some current items of interest in the news.

They could tell you about times when they brought evil into their own world by the way in which they used their gifts or talents. Read or tell the children the story of the Fall from the Book of Genesis. Reflect with them on the meaning of the story. Talk to them about the symbolism of the serpent and the forbidden fruit.

7. If you wish to spend some time praying with the children, you could reflect with them on God's call to all of us to use our gifts and talents creatively to make the world a better place, and on the fact that we often choose to follow the way of evil rather

than of love and so fail to answer God's call. Then read with them Psalm 31 from p. 16 of the pupil's book.

UNIT 2
WORKERS FOR A BETTER WORLD

In this unit we explore further with the children, in concrete terms, the concept of working for a better world. We do this by introducing them to stories of people who spent/spend their lives working in various ways to make the world a better place. We use stories of people from the Old Testament, from history and from the present day.

The lessons in this unit are:

Moses works for a better world
David and Solomon work for a better world
People of vision work for a better world
People today continue to work for a better world

CLASSROOM VISITATION LINKED TO UNIT 2

In this unit the children hear the stories of seven people who used their gifts and talents to make the world a better place — Moses; David; Solomon; Nano Nagle; Mahatma Gandhi; Willie Bermingham. You could encourage the children to tell you stories they have heard from the lives of any of these people. You could then reflect with them on the qualities which the person in the story showed: courage, perseverance, wisdom etc; the difficulties which faced them: opposition, persecution, self-sacrifice etc; the things which made it possible for them to do as they did: help from others, the assurance they had that they were doing God's will, their belief that God was with them, the help which they got from others etc.

2. On pp.170-175 of the teacher's book you will find a penance service for the season of Advent which prepares the children for a celebration of the Sacrament of Penance in the context of the programme. You may like to take part in this with the teachers and the children.

UNIT 3
JESUS WORKS FOR A BETTER WORLD AS HE ANNOUNCES THE KINGDOM

This unit concentrates on the life and message of Jesus. Central to the teaching of Jesus is the Kingdom of God. Love is the law of the Kingdom. The Sermon on the Mount tells us the values of the Kingdom. In order to enter the Kingdom we must take seriously Jesus' call to repentance and conversion.

The lessons in this unit are:

At Christmas we celebrate the coming of Jesus
Learning about the Bible
Jesus announces the Kingdom which is for all people
Jesus' Kingdom is where people serve one another and show respect
Jesus' Kingdom here on earth is where people live by truth, justice, peace and love
The teaching of Jesus shows us how to work for the Kingdom
Jesus helped people to be better workers for the Kingdom by teaching them that God was Father, Son and Holy Spirit
Jesus calls us to repent
Jesus invites us to work for the Kingdom today

CLASSROOM VISITATION LINKED TO UNIT 3

1.   The first lesson in this unit is a lesson on Christmas. The children will enjoy either listening to or telling the story of the birth of Jesus. They may also have prepared a Christmas play or project. You could invite them to perform the play for you or to tell you about the project. They have examined the origins of certain Christmas customs: the crib; the singing of carols; holly; the Christmas tree. You could encourage them to sing for you some of the Christmas carols they have learned.

2.   In the second lesson of the unit we concentrate on giving the children some factual information about the New Testament: how it was written, what it contains etc. We tell them that it was first written on papyrus sheets, later on parchment and vellum scrolls, and was printed for the first time in 1440 by John Gutenberg. We also talk about the Book of Kells, the Book of Durrow and the Book of Armagh. You could encourage the children to tell you about the different kinds of books in the New

Testament. Talk to them about the different times when you use the New Testament and about why you see it as an important book.

3. Encourage the children to tell you stories which show that Jesus tried to improve the conditions in which people lived — not just some people but all people. They concentrate in this unit on the story of the Great Feast and of the woman in the house of Simon. But you could also revise with them stories they have learned in earlier classes: Amos; Bartimaeus; Zacchaeus; the sinner woman. The programme also tells a story of an incident from the life of Don Bosco where he helped a poor boy whom nobody else cared for. You might like to ask them to tell you this story. You could also tell them stories from your experience of incidents where someone worked to change the situations of others so that they could live more fully.

4. You could read with the children the story 'The Hunter' from p. 39 of the pupil's book. This should lead to discussion on the beauty of the world of nature and the need to treat it with respect and reverence. You could ask the children to talk about some of the things they have learned about Jesus which show that he treated the world with respect and reverence. Ask them to talk about things they do which show respect for the world and about things they do which fail to show respect for the world.

On pp. 225-27 of the teacher's book there is a number of short stories illustrating the call to respect ourselves and others and the difficulties sometimes involved in making that choice. Ask the children to talk about things Jesus did which show the respect he had for other people. Talk to the children about the 4th, 5th, 6th and 9th commandments and about what is forbidden and commanded by these.

5. You could read the story 'Catherine and the Winter Wheat' from pp. 42 and 43 of the pupil's book. This story illustrates the call to live with others in truth, justice, peace and love and the difficulty that is sometimes involved in choosing to do this. Encourage the children to talk about incidents from their own lives when they had to choose whether or not to be truthful and honest, whether to build peace instead of conflict, whether or not to respect the rights of others.

You could tell them a similar story from your own experience. You could ask them to tell you the 7th, 8th and 10th commandments and what is forbidden and commanded by these.

If you wish to pray with the children you could use the prayerful reflection on p. 45 of the pupil's book.

6.   The lesson commencing on p. 46 of the pupil's book introduces the children to the teaching of Jesus in the Sermon on the Mount. You could read the extracts with the children and encourage them to talk about ways in whch they could put each into practice in their own lives. You could read the Beatitudes with the children, again reflecting on the meaning of each. You could link this with the prayerful reflection on p. 49 of the pupil's book.

There is also a poem entitled 'The Beatitudes' on p. 49 of the pupil's book which is worth reading slowly and reflectively.

7.   In this unit we introduce the childen to the mystery of the Blessed Trinity. We try to help them to understand something of the relationship which Jesus had with the Father and with the Spirit. You could talk to them about some of the times when we show honour and respect for the Blessed Trinity: when we make the Sign of the Cross; when we pray the Apostles' Creed; when we pray the Glory be to the Father; when we make the Sign of the Cross on the baby's head at baptism.

You could also talk to them about the ways in which each person of the Trinity helps us. Encourage them to talk to you about the first three commandments and about what is forbidden and commanded by them.

8.   On pp.209-276 of the teacher's book the structure of the Sacrament of Reconciliation Rite I and Rite II is developed for use with the children. In the context of this programme you will also find a penance service for Lent on pp.288-92. The gospel story used to help the children come to a deeper understanding of the love and mercy of God is the story of the prodigal son.

You could help the children to prepare for the Sacrament of Reconciliation by telling the story of the prodigal son and reflecting on it with them. You could also use some of the text on pp.267 and 268 of the teacher's book to help the children to examine their consciences in the light of what they have learned in this unit.

9.   In the last lesson in the unit we explore with the children the ways in which they can, in the context of the opportunities that present themselves in the ordinary course of their daily lives, be workers for the Kingdom. This lesson is a summary of the entire unit.

You could ask the children to talk about things which they have done or could do which would help to make the world a better place for themselves and for the people with whom they live and play and learn.

You could also ask the children to list the ten commandments and to say what each means for them in their daily lives.

UNIT 4
THE RISEN JESUS HELPS US TO WORK FOR THE KINGDOM

In this unit we help the children to reflect again on the significance of the death and resurrection of Jesus. We help them to see that Jesus worked to build a Kingdom of love and continued to do that in spite of opposition and hatred. Because of his love for the Father and his love for others, he gave himself totally to his mission in life and in death. The Father responded to Jesus by raising him to new life in the resurrection. We help the children to come to a deeper understanding of the ongoing presence of the risen Jesus with us, particularly in the sacraments, helping us we continue his work of building a Kingdom.

The lessons in this unit are:

Jesus works for the Kingdom by giving his life for us
At Mass we join with the risen Jesus as he continues to give himself to the Father
We work for the Kingdom when we celebrate the presence of the risen Jesus at Mass
In the sacraments the risen Jesus helps us to work for the Kingdom of God
Jesus is Lord

CLASSROOM VISITATION LINKED TO UNIT 4

1.   You might like to help the children to reflect again on the stories of the death and resurrection of Jesus.

You could do this by telling or by reading the stories for them, or, alternatively, they could tell you the stories. The resurrection story for this year is from John 21 and the aspect of the death of Jesus that we concentrate on is the suffering of Jesus which he endured because of his love for God and for the people around him.

You could help the children to reflect on suffering in their own lives and in the lives of people around them in order to help them to understand better the suffering of Jesus. They could talk about sickness, death in their families, missing their friends, loneliness, being left out of games etc.

Starting on p.300 of the teacher's book you will find reflections for the Stations of the Cross which were prepared in the context of the Fifth Class/Primary 7 programme. You might like to use them to make the Stations of the Cross with the children either in the church, if this is convenient, or in the classroom.

2.   We introduce the children to the notion of sacrifice as giving oneself for others. They are helped to understand the concept of sacrifice in a concrete way through the story of Oscar Romero and a poem, 'The present', which speaks of love as the 'best gift' which we can give to others. Encourage the children to think about the ways in whch they can give themselves to and for others.

Talk to the children about Mass as a time when we remember and make present the sacrifice of Jesus. Remind them of the way in which he told his followers at the Last Supper that we too must be prepared to give ourselves for others and that at Mass the risen Jesus gives himself to us to enable us to live as he asks us. Encourage them to tell you the story of the disciples on the road to Emmaus.

3.   On p. 66 of the pupil's book you will find a list of things we do at Mass. You could ask the children to talk about each of these. On p.32 of the teacher's book there is the text for a class Mass for Fifth Class/Primary 7. You might like to prepare and celebrate Mass in the classroom with the teacher and the children. It is important that the children be involved to the fullest possible extent in the preparation of the Mass, in choosing the readings etc. It is important to link the actual celebration of the Mass with the theory they have learned. In this way it can become a real learning experience for the children which should help them to understand better what happens at Mass in the parish church on Sundays.

4.   Encourage the children to talk about the different ways in which God is present to us: in the world; in Jesus; in the community of the Church; in the seven sacraments.

You could also ask the children to list the seven sacraments and to name those events from life which are celebrated in each one.

On p. 68 of the pupil's book there is a scripture text relating to each of the sacraments and a key phrase from the rite. You could talk with the children about the content of this page.

5. You could read the text of Acts 2:43-47 and encourage the children to talk about the way in whch the early Christians lived. Encourage them to talk about how the early Christians came to the firm belief that the risen Jesus was with them. Talk to them about the fact that the risen Jesus is also present with us. Encourage them to sing the hymn 'He is Lord'.

UNIT 5

THE COMMUNITY OF THE CHURCH WORK TOGETHER FOR THE KINGDOM

In this unit we help the children to understand more fully that when we were baptised we became members of the community of the Church, the people who work together to create in this world the conditions by which Jesus characterised the Kingdom: a place where there is truth, justice, peace and love.

In Baptism we received the Holy Spirit for the first time and in Confirmation we receive the fullness of the Spirit, who helps us as we try to work with the community of the Church to build the Kingdom.

The lessons in this unit are:

Working together in the Church
The risen Jesus sends the Holy Spirit to his followers
In Confirmation we celebrate the gift of the Holy Spirit
The Sacrament of Confirmation Living as workers for the Kingdom
Mary the Mother of Jesus
Living in the Kingdom forever

CLASSROOM VISITATION LINKED TO UNIT 5

1. Encourage the children to talk about times when they worked together with others as a team. Help them to discuss some of the things that are necessary for good teamwork. Talk to them about the parish as a team working together to create a better world.

Talk to them about instances in your parish where groups of people worked together on a project, e.g. sale of work; parish sports day; fund-raising event; old folks' party etc. Encourage them to tell you ways in which they can work for the good of the parish.

You could talk to them about the different roles people have in the Church, e.g. bishops, priests, parents, children etc, and about the ways in which all of these are complementary and can work together so that the work of the Church can be done most effectively. You might like to use the prayerful reflection on p. 72 of the pupil's book as a starting point for prayer with the children.

2. The children have heard the story of the coming of the Holy Spirit on the apostles at Pentecost and the story from Acts 3:4 about Peter and John at the temple. You could encourage them to talk about the effect the Holy Spirit had on the lives of the apostles. Perhaps they might like to act out the Pentecost story. There is a prayer service on p. 369 of the teacher's book which you might like to use with the children as Pentecost Sunday draws close.

3. In this unit there are two lessons on the Sacrament of Confirmation. It is recommended that these lessons are taught to children in Fifth Class/Primary 7 only if they are celebrating the Sacrament of Confirmation.

In the text for Sixth Class/First Year Post-Primary there will be notes for a special visit before Confirmation. If, in your situation, children are celebrating the sacrament of Confirmation in Primary 7 or in Fifth Class you will find these notes helpful.

4. Encourage the children to talk about different ways in which people work for the Kingdom in the world today: the St Vincent de Paul society; meals on wheels; ALONE; CASA etc. Encourage them to tell you specific things they have done or can do. You could tell them about the things which you do. Encourage them to sing the hymn 'Here I am Lord'.

5. We help the children to think about some of the things which Jesus said we must do in order to reach the Kingdom of God. They have heard the parable of the hidden treasure, the parable of the pearl, the parable of the great feast. You could encourage the children to tell you these stories and to discuss them.

You could read for them the passage from Matthew 25 which you can find on p. 421 of the teacher's book and talk with them about its meaning.

Encourage them to ask questions about this. Encourage them to tell you the story of Alfred Nobel and the story of the Dragon Fly which they will have heard (p. 422 teacher's book). Reflect with them on the meaning of these stories.

VISIT FOR THE MONTH OF MAY

1. Encourage the children to tell you what they know about the life of Mary as she grew up. They could also tell you the stories of the Annunciation and the Visitation. You could talk to them about Mary's great suffering as she watched her son often rejected by the people and finally put to death by crucifixion. Talk to them about the ways in which Mary is honoured in the Church. Ask them to name the mysteries of the Rosary.

2. You could gather with them round the May altar for the prayer service which is included on p. 85 of the pupil's book.

SIXTH CLASS/FIRST YEAR POST-PRIMARY

Pupil's Book: *Called to Serve* (Republic of Ireland and Britain)
I will be with you (Northern Ireland and Britain)

Teacher's Book: *Walk in my Presence*

Background to the approach in the Sixth Class/First Year Post-Primary programme

The theme of this year's programme is communication. We help the children to reflect upon and explore their experience of speaking and listening, calling and responding. In the light of this experience we help them to see that God speaks to us continually and invites us to enter into a relationship of love with him. We present the different ways in which God speaks to us: in the world; through people; through the Bible; through Jesus; in the sacraments. We help them to see that God has given us free will and so we can choose to respond to his call or we can choose to ignore it.

UNIT 1
GOD SPEAKS TO US

In this unit we start by helping the children to become more aware of the people and things around them. We encourage them to be more sensitive to other people, to listen more carefully to them when they try to communicate and to have respect for their feelings. We try to develop in them an appreciation for the values of love, care, co-operation, inter-dependence, respect, trust, honesty, truthfulness. We also encourage them to look with greater appreciation and respect at the world around them and to become aware that, because it was created by God, we can see there signs of the care, power, grandeur and love of God.

The lessons in this unit are:

We communicate
Listening to and telling stories
God speaks to us through people
God speaks to us in the world around us

CLASSROOM VISITATION LINKED TO UNIT 1

1. You might like to welcome the children back to school and, if appropriate, to refer to the fact that they are the senior students in the school this year and that therefore people will look to them to show good example to those younger, to be extra helpful, to take on more responsibility in and around the school.

You could also, where appropriate, refer to the fact that during this year they will prepare for and celebrate the Sacrament of Confirmation. Assure them that you would like to offer them all the help and support possible during their preparation.

2. Encourage the children to talk about the different ways in which we can communicate with one another: spoken word; gesture; written word; giving gifts.

They will also talk about the variety that is possible within each of these, e.g. words of anger, words of love, words of sorrow, questioning words etc. You could encourage them to give examples of times when they would use each.

Talk to them about the fact that communication is a two-way process and involves listening and responding as well as speaking. Help them to become more aware of the fact that we can choose whether or not to respond to those around us. You could tell them stories about times when you responded to something you heard, perhaps someone looking for help, or perhaps an invitation to attend a paricular function and also about times when you refused to listen or respond. You could encourage them to tell you about times when they responded to their parents, their teacher, their friends and about times they chose not to respond.

3. Encourage the children to tell you the Legend of the Rainbow. Encourage them to talk about the truth contained in this story. You could use the following questions: Have you ever seen the kind of situation the story talks about happen in real life? Why did the colours act as they did? Have you ever acted as the colours did in the story? Have you ever seen a situation

where people co-operated as the colours were urged to do in the story?

4. Encourage the children to tell the story of Helen Keller or anyone else whose life was such that, through it God's care, love and compassion was reflected for others. You could tell them a story about such a person.

5. Read with the children the version of Psalm 28 which you will find on p. 8 of the pupil's book.
Talk to them about ways in which the beauty of the earth speaks to you of God. Encourage them to talk to you about their own appreciation of the earth.

6. You could use the prayerful reflection on p. 9 of the pupil's book as a starting point for prayer with the children before you leave. You could encourage the children to add their own spontaneous prayers. They may also like to sing one of the hymns they have learned in this unit: 'Yahweh I know you are near', or 'I will never forget you'.

UNIT 2
GOD CALLS US TO FRIENDSHIP WITH HIM

The first lesson in this unit helps the children to gain some factual information about the Bible, especially the Old Testament, how it was written and what it contains. It also tries to convey to them a sense of reverence for the Bible and encourages them to see it as the word of God. The remainder of the unit takes a similar approach to that in Unit 2 of the programme 'Workers for the Kingdom'. We present the stories of nine people ranging from biblical times to the present day, each of whom responded 'Yes' to God's call.

The lessons in this unit are:

God calls his people in the Old Testament
Abraham and Moses say 'Yes' to God's call
Elijah and Jeremiah say 'Yes' to God's call
John the Baptist says 'Yes' to God's call
People have always heard God's call and said 'Yes'
People today say 'Yes' to God's call

CLASSROOM VISITATION LINKED TO UNIT 2

1. Encourage the children to tell you the facts they know about the Bible and about the Old Testament in particular — the ways in which it was written down through the ages, the types of book it contains, what it tries to convey etc. Talk to the children about the times you use parts of the Old Testament and explain why.

2. Encourage the children to tell you stories of the lives of any of the people dealt with in Unit 2: Moses; Abraham; Elijah; Jeremiah; Martin Luther King; John the Baptist; Vincent de Paul; Mary Aikenhead; Mother Teresa of Calcutta.

Encourage them to reflect on the ways in which these people heard God speak to them. Reflect with them on the fact that very often they had to endure suffering, pain and rejection in order to respond to God's call.

It took great courage and perseverance on their part to continue, in spite of the difficulties. They were, however, aware that God was with them and this enabled them to continue to respond. Help them to relate the content of this unit to their own lives. You could ask them: When or where does God call you? When do you find it difficult to respond to his call? What helps you to respond? Remind them that in the Sacrament of Confirmation they will receive the fullness of the gift of the Holy Spirit to give them the strength they need to hear and answer God's call as it comes to them in their own lives.

3. You could use the prayerful reflection on p.25 of the pupil's book as a starting point to help you to pray with the children. Encourage them to add their own spontaneous prayers. They could also sing one of the hymns in this unit: 'If God is for us'; 'Song for a young prophet'; 'Abba Father'; 'I will be with you'; 'Here I am Lord'.

5. On p.155 of the teacher's book you will find a prayer service of commitment which marks a stage in the children's preparation for Confirmation. It also helps to alert the parents to their role in helping the children live up to their Confirmation commitment. You might like to take part in this prayer service with the children, the parents and the teacher. The most appropriate setting for this prayer service is probably the parish church and the most appropriate time is an evening when the parents would be free to attend.

UNIT 3
JESUS IS THE WORD OF GOD

In this unit we help the children to come to know that it is in Jesus, above all, that God communicates with us. Jesus is the word of God. In him we see clearly the love, justice, mercy and compassion of God in action. Jesus also reveals the mystery of God's inner life, and we help the children to deepen their understanding of the mystery of the Trinity. We help the children to come to know Jesus more fully through prayer and through the New Testament. Gospel stories, sayings, parables and miracles are selected which help the children to grasp how Jesus revealed the mystery of God and his love for all people.

The lessons in this unit are:

Jesus grows up
Jesus helps us to understand the love and forgiveness of God
At Christmas we celebrate the birth of Jesus
Jesus helps us to understand the love and justice of God
The risen Jesus calls us to be one

CLASSROOM VISITATION LINKED TO UNIT 3

1. The children have been presented with some geographical and historical facts about the country where Jesus grew up as well as some information about the customs of the people. You could ask them to talk to you about the life of Jesus as a child, the things he may have seen and done and the people with whom he associated.

If you have visited Israel you may like to talk to them about your visit or perhaps you have some pictures or slides which you could show them.

2. In the context of Advent the programme includes a penance service and a text for the celebration of the Sacrament of Reconciliation for children. In a lesson on the love and forgiveness of God we help the children to reflect on the stages in the process of reconciliation. You could ask the children to talk about times when they experienced being forgiven. You could also tell them about a similar experience from your own life. They could tell you a story about forgiveness entitled 'Raven Boy and Little Hawk', which is included in the programme. We help them to understand the nature of God's forgiveness through

reflecting with them on some stories of forgiveness from the gospel. The gospel stories about forgiveness in this programme are Jesus in the house of Simon the Pharisee, The lost sheep, The lost son, The lost coin, The parable of the unforgiving servant. You could ask the children to tell any of these stories and then discuss with them the aspects of reconciliation that we can see in action in each story.

You may also like to prepare with the teacher and the children for the celebration of a penance service and of the Sacrament of Reconciliation. You will find the text of the penance service commencing on p. 170 of the teacher's book and of the Sacrament of Reconcilation on p. 189.

3. In the Christmas lesson we help the children to appreciate that Christmas can be a very difficult time for people who are poor or who are suffering sadness of one kind or another.

You could ask the children to tell you the story entitled 'Visiting hour', which talks about the experience of a young boy from a very poor family, who brings a Christmas cake to his father who was in prison because he stole a hen in order to feed his hungry family.

We encourage the children to think about how they can celebrate the birth of Jesus today in a world where there is still much poverty and suffering. You could talk to the children about this and encourage them to make their own suggestions.

You could ask the children to sing some of the carols they have learned from countries around the globe. They may also have prepared a Christmas play or pageant which you might like to see. Alternatively, you could encourage them to tell you the story of the birth of Jesus at Christmas.

4. In this unit we help the children to reflect on some of the qualities of the justice of God. You could encourage them to reflect with you on the scripture stories which they hear in the programme: Workers in the vineyard, The widow's treasure. You may also like to reflect with them on the story 'The coming of the King' which is included on p.35 of the pupil's book. The following questions may help to start a discussion on the story. Who was looked upon as being 'important' in the town? Who did the King see as being important in the town? How does the town in the story compare with our town or parish? Does this story remind you of any of the stories which Jesus told?

5. You might like to use the prayerful reflection on p.224 of the teacher's book as a starting point for prayer with the children.

6. This unit also includes a supplementary lesson for the celebration of the Church Unity Octave. The lesson includes stories of ways in which Christians in Ireland today work together for unity. You could talk to them about ways in which this happens in the part of the country where you live. You could also take part with the teacher and children in the prayer service for Christian unity which is included on p.233 of the teacher's book.

UNIT 4
JESUS SHOWS US HOW TO RESPOND

This unit concentrates on moral development. We reflect with the children on how they should respect the world, themselves, other people and God. Jesus not only revealed God to us but showed us how we should respond to God. He did this in his own life by his actions and words, in the way in which he related to other people, to the world and to God. When we refuse to respond to other people and to God as Jesus taught us, or when we refuse to look upon the world with the respect he asked of us, we sin. God's forgiveness is always available to us, especially in the Sacrament of Reconciliation. We deal with the commandments in the different lessons of this unit but we do so in the light of the teaching of Jesus. In this unit there is a section which has been included to help a teacher, who so wishes, to deal with sex education. It is not intended that this material be done merely as a matter of course and the programme clearly states that it should always be done in consultation with parents.

The lessons in this unit are:

Respecting the world
Respecting ourselves and others
Responding to the needs of others
Respecting God
Responding to the word of God

CLASSROOM VISITATION LINKED TO UNIT 4

You could ask the children to tell you the story of 'The Hook' which is included on p. 38 of their own book. Alternatively, you could read it with them. Discuss with them the issue raised in this story — the cruelty with which some poeple treat birds and animals. You could then broaden the discussion to include the question of how people should treat the world around them in general. Encourage them to tell you ways in which they can treat the world with the appropriate respect and ways in which they can mistreat the world. You could talk to them about the example Jesus showed us in his own care for the world (see p.251 teacher's book). You could read slowly and reflectively with the children Psalm 65 from p.39 of their own books.

2. Encourage the children to talk about the uniqueness of each individual person and the reasons why they deserve to be treated with respect. You could ask them to tell you some of the rights that each person has. The following are mentioned in the programme: to life; to be different; to the truth; to reasonable comfort; to property. You could ask them to tell either of the two life experience stories in this lesson, 'The story of David' or 'The pencil box'.

Reflect with them on the story of 'The woman caught in adultery' which shows the way in which Jesus respected all people. You could also encourage the children to talk about the 4th, 5th, 6th and 9th commandments which the programme deals with in this context. They will be able to tell you what is commanded and forbidden by each. You can encourage them to relate this to their own experience of life.

You could read with the children the version of Psalm 8 which is included on p. 42 of their own books and reflect with them on the meaning of the psalm.

3. Encourage the children to talk about the different needs that people experience, people in your own locality, people throughout the country, people in the broader world. You could help them to give examples from relevant newspaper and television reports. You could ask them if they can think of ways in which they can respond to any of these needs. In helping the children to think again about the way in which Jesus responded to the needs of others we reflect with them on the following stories: The widow's son; The good samaritan; The feeding of the five thousand. They could tell any of these stories and you

could then discuss the stories with the entire class. They could sing the hymn 'Whatsoever you do'. In this context also you could discuss with them the 7th, 8th and 10th commandments.

Jesus showed us how to respect God by the example of his own life and death. You could talk to the children about the ways in which Jesus showed respect for God.

You could encourage them to tell you about the time when Jesus taught the Our Father to his followers and help them to reflect on the meaning of the different phrases in the Our Father. Encourage the children to tell you and to talk about the story of the pharisee and the tax collector. You could also talk with the children about the first three commandments in this context.

5. This programme revises the Sermon on the Mount including the Beatitudes which have already been covered in detail in the Fifth Class/Primary 7 programme. You could encourage the children to say the Beatitudes together and then to talk about the meaning of each. In the programme, they are helped to understand the Beatitudes by linking the quality spoken of in each to the life of someone who showed that quality in action. We help them to think about the difficulty that we sometimes experience in trying to respond to the word of God. They could tell you the story of 'The rich young man' or 'The parable of the sower'. Through use of the examination of conscience which is included on p. 310 of the teacher's book you could help the children to look at ways in their own lives in which they fail to respond to the word of God. It is important also to help them to become more aware of the fact that the forgiveness of God is always available to us when we recognise that we have failed and try to listen and respond to God's call to us in our lives. You may also like to take part with them in the penance service for Lent which is included in the teacher's text, starting on p.313.

UNIT 5
JESUS IS RAISED TO NEW LIFE

In this unit we help the children to understand more fully the death and resurrection of Jesus. The death of Jesus shows us that Jesus responded in his life to God's call even to the point of death and the resurrection of Jesus shows us that God responded to him by raising him to new life. We help them to be aware that, as followers of Jesus, they too are challenged to respond to God's call in their lives even when it leads to hardship and suffering.

The lessons in this unit are:

Jesus dies on the cross
Jesus is raised to new life
The followers of the risen Jesus come to see God as Father, Son and Holy Spirit

CLASSROOM VISITATION LINKED TO UNIT 5

1.   Encourage the children to reflect on their own suffering, e.g. illness, death of a family member etc. Encourage them also to think of times when they are prepared to suffer for the sake of others, or they could give examples of instances which show that people they have contact with are prepared to suffer for them, e.g. parents may be prepared to do without new clothes so that their children can have a better education etc.

Encourage them to give examples from the programme of people who suffered because they were determined to answer God's call to bring his love to all people, e.g. Mother Teresa, Vincent de Paul etc.

You could read with the children the story of the passion, or, alternatively, you could encourage them to tell you the story as they remember it. The teacher's book includes a text for the Stations of the Cross which is suitable for children. If appropriate, you could take the children to the local church to make the Stations of the Cross using this text as a basis.

2.   You could encourage the children to talk about the way in which we experience new life in the earth in springtime.

Talk to the children about the way in which God the Father responded to the sacrifice of Jesus by raising him to new life in the resurrection. The resurrection story that the children concentrate on in this class is the story of Jesus and Thomas. You could also help them to recall the other resurrection stories that they have heard in previous programmes.

3.   Talk to the children about the way in which each person of the Trinity relates to us and helps us.

You could use the prayer in the lesson on the Trinity on p. 5 of the pupil's book as a starting point for prayer with the children.

UNIT 6
THE MASS

In this unit we help the children to come to a deeper appreciation and understanding of the Mass. We revise and expand on much of the material that has already been covered in earlier programmes. We present the Mass as the action of the risen Jesus and of the people of God. We help the children to appreciate the different aspects of the Mass: celebration; meal; memorial; thanksgiving; sacrifice; communion with Christ; sacrifice of Christ's presence.

The lessons in this unit are:

At Mass we celebrate the presence of the risen Jesus
At Mass we join with the risen Jesus as he continues to give himself to the Father
At Mass we give thanks to God with the risen Jesus
The Mass through the centuries

CLASSROOM VISITATION LINKED TO UNIT 6

One of the best and most important ways in which you can link in with the work of this unit is through the preparation of and celebration of a class Mass with the teacher and children. It is important that the children be involved on as high a level as possible in both the preparation of and celebration of this Mass. The teacher may feel the need of your support. The children could choose appropriate hymns from those they have learned in the programme. At the Penitential Rite you could encourage them to mention specific examples of ways in which they have failed. They could help choose the readings. They could make up their own prayers of the faithful and be involved in the presentation of the gifts at the Offertory.

You could use the Children's Eucharistic Prayer which is dealt with in the programme. In both the preparation and celebration of the Mass you could help the children to understand more fully the two central points which are emphasised in this year's programme: (i) that the risen Jesus is present with us at Mass in the people, in the word, in the priest, in the consecrated bread and wine and (ii) that at Mass the risen Jesus continues to give himself to the Father and to us.

CONFIRMATION

In the programme we help the children to understand their Confirmation as a time when they celebrate the fact that they have completed a certain part of their growth in faith. Their parents, teachers and priests recognise that this growth has taken place and gather with the bishop to celebrate it. We also help them to understand that in Confirmation they receive the fullness of the gift of the Holy Spirit which they received for the first time in Baptism. We help them to reflect on the action of the Holy Spirit in their lives by reflecting on the story of Pentecost, the story of Stephen and other incidents from the lives of the early Christians, as well as by helping them to reflect on the obvious qualities in the lives of those through whom the Spirit is at work. We help them to understand the gifts and fruits of the Holy Spirit through linking the abstract concepts to the qualities that we perceive in the lives of people. We look again at those people with whom we dealt in the earlier part of the programme, e.g. Mary Aikenhead, Mother Teresa etc. and also people in the actual day-to-day experience of the children who show qualities of courage, wisdom, understanding etc. in action, and through whom others can experience love, joy, peace and patience etc. In line with the overall theme of this year's programme, 'call and response', we help the children to realise that in Confirmation God is calling them to take a more active, more mature role in the Church. We help them to come to a deeper understanding of the Church as 'the people of God', that each person has a role in the Church and that the work of the Church can be done best only when each one plays their part.

CLASSROOM VISITATION LINKED TO CONFIRMATION

You might make a number of visits to the classroom as Confirmation draws near and you can choose from the following topics:

1.   Talk to the children about the local Church in your parish. Help them to see the many ways in which different people play their part. Reflect with them on the fact that things happen so much more easily when people co-operate and when each one is allowed to use his or her particular gifts and talents for the sake of all. Encourage them to think of things they can do in the local community which would be of help to others. You could

ask them to tell you the story of 'The two brothers' which is included in the text of the pupil's book. Reflect with them on the meaning of this story in relation to the things that happen in your own parish.

2. Encourage the children to talk to you about the mission that Jesus gave to his followers — they have heard the story of 'The sending out of the twelve' and 'The sending out of the seventy-two'.

You could tell the children the story of the coming of the Holy Spirit at Pentecost, emphasising the ways in which the apostles were influenced by this event. They may like to dramatise this story for you. You could also ask them to tell you the story of Stephen. Encourage them to talk about the way in which the early Christians lived, e.g. Acts 2:44-47. Encourage them to discuss the reasons why the early Christians lived according to this particular lifestyle.

3. Talk to the children about the fact that since they first received the Holy Spirit in Baptism they have been growing and learning. They are now able to do many things that they could not have done at an earlier age. They are able to contribute more and more to the lives of those around them. They have developed their gifts and talents. They have heard the story of Jesus and know more about what is asked of them, as his followers, in the world today. The Holy Spirit has been with them, helping them as they have grown and learned.

Talk to them about Confirmation as a time when this growth is acknowledged and celebrated. It is also the time when they receive the fullness of the gift of the Holy Spirit who will be with them helping them and guiding them as they play an even bigger part in the work of the Church in their homes, at school and in the local parish. Encourage them to name for you the seven gifts of the Holy Spirit and to try to explain how these gifts can influence our lives when we work to become the kind of people that God wants us to be.

It is important to help them to understand that the gifts of the Holy Spirit do not make magical changes in our lives, that the Holy Spirit is the one who helps us as we try to become more and more the kind of person that we are called to be.

They can be helped to understand this more clearly through examples from people's lives, e.g. Abraham had to risk leaving his own home. It was difficult, but because he was determined to do as God had asked him the Holy Spirit gave him the courage he needed.

You could help the children to talk about the fruits of the Holy Spirit by encouraging them to talk about people whose lives show the fruits of the Holy Spirit in action. They can recall the lives of people about whom they have already learned in the programme, e.g. Jeremiah, Vincent de Paul etc. They can also give examples from the lives of people around them, e.g. the kindness of the teacher, their parents etc.

You could also encourage the children to talk about the symbolism used in connection with the Holy Spirit — wind, breath, fire.

You could use the prayer-reflection on p. 78 of the pupil's book as a starting point for prayer with the children.

4. It would probably be helpful both for the children and for the teacher if you talked to the children about the various parts of the Rite of Confirmation, the actions and symbols used and their significance.

5. Encourage the children to talk about the ways in which they can respond in their lives to the call of God in Confirmation. Encourage them to give actual practical examples of opportunities which present themselves in their experience, where they can either take up the challenge to live as followers of Jesus, or they can ignore God's call and refuse to do this. You could give examples of ways in which people in the parish, in groups, or as individuals are already doing this, e.g. the members of the St Vincent de Paul Society, those who organise meals-on-wheels etc. You could broaden this discussion to include a missionary dimension by asking the children to talk about people who answered God's call to bring his love to those who live in distant parts of the world, people from Irish history such as Thomas Quinlan or St Gall or people you know who are the missionaries of the present day. You could use the prayerful reflection on p. 82 of the pupil's book as a starting point for prayer with the children.

CLASSROOM VISITATION FOR THE MONTH OF MAY

1. Encourage the children to tell you all they can about Mary, the country where she grew up, her early years, her role as the Mother of Jesus.

2. You could talk to the children about the role of Mary in the Church — the feast days in her honour and what is celebrated on each.

3. You could ask them to name the different places of pilgrimage in honour of Mary. If any of them have visited any of these places they could tell about the visit. Alternatively, you could talk to them about a pilgrimage you took part in to Lourdes, Knock etc.

4. If the children have not made a May altar in the classroom you could encourage them to do so. If they have you could gather them around the May altar for a prayer in honour of Mary. An appropriate prayer for this occasion might be one of the joyful mysteries of the Rosary. Encourage the children to talk about the story from the life of Mary which is being celebrated in this mystery. They could also sing some of the hymns they have learned in honour of Mary.

ADDITIONAL RESOURCES

The following publications provide additional material which you may find useful in your work with children in primary school.

Children of God Series pupil and teacher books from Junior Infants/Primary 1 to Sixth class/First Year Post-Primary.
Let's Celebrate, which provides a text for the celebration of First Confession and First Holy Communion
Masses for Children by Sr Francesca Kelly
More Masses for Children by Sr Francesca Kelly
Leading our Children to God by Fr Sean Melody
The Columba Lectionary for Masses with Children
Praise! (Lion Publications) is a book of Psalms translated for children
Listen! (Lion Publications) is a book of Gospel stories translated for children